I QUIT!

I QUIT!

Confessions of an Imperfect Homeschool Mom

TIFFANY WASSON

XULON PRESS

Xulon Press
2301 Lucien Way #415
Maitland, FL 32751
407.339.4217
www.xulonpress.com

Paperback ISBN-13: 978-1-6628-4352-5
Dust Jacket ISBN-13: 978-1-6628-4353-2
eBook ISBN-13: 978-1-6628-4430-0

Endorsements

"Tiffany opens the door and invites the reader into her home-school journey. Her honest confessions resonate with me even in my 25th year of homeschooling. With a combination of journal-style writing, tips, scripture, and resources, this book will be a welcome handbook to parents, especially those who need to know they are not alone in the trenches."

Susan Schaeffer, Homeschool Mom of 25 Years

"Calling all homeschool moms! If you need a boost in morale, wisdom, and encouragement to keep you pushing through these homeschool years, this book is for you! Reading this book feels like sitting down with a friend and gleaning wisdom and encouragement over a hot cup of coffee!"

Haley Valencia, Homeschool Mom of 10 Years

Table of Contents

To our boys, Aaron and Austin, you are my sunshines.
I love you more!

Introduction

If you had told me at eighteen that I would get married, have two kids, and homeschool them, I would have laughed hysterically. Or I would have shouted, "Get behind me, Satan!" See, when I was eighteen, I was young, driven, and I was chomping at the bit to join the ministry. I wanted to travel, speak, and teach from the stage. I did not see myself with kids—and definitely not as a housewife or homeschool mom. I was ready for the world, with Jesus in my heart and by my side.

Well, you may have heard this precious gem of scripture tucked away in Proverbs 16:9 which says, "A man's heart plans his way, but the LORD determines his steps." Yeah, that's what happened to me. I thought I knew where I was headed in life, but I was seriously wrong. Not long after I graduated high school, I found the man of my dreams and my life was forever changed. I won't bore you with all the mushy details—that's in another book—but after we got married, we had two handsome boys.

As a family, we have been on some crazy life roller coasters and one of the biggest ones we've endured is homeschooling our kids. Our journey started about nine years ago and it's been a wild ride; a heart beating faster, stomach aching, rush-to-the-brain kind of wild. However, it turns out the ride I never thought I'd step foot on just happens to be my favorite—but it didn't start out that way.

These are my confessions.

CONFESSION #1

I Did Not Want to Homeschool Our Kids

repeat. I did not want to homeschool our kids.

I had actually tried it once before when our boys were four and two. Obviously, the two-year-old wasn't school-aged, but I was determined to help him learn as much as he could. I had read all the blogs and articles that talked about the fact that children's brains grow up to 90 percent capacity by age five, so no one was getting saved by the bell—school was about to be in session.

Call me crazy and a little overzealous but I only have two speeds: lazy, and obsessed. At this particular moment in time, I was obviously obsessed. I wanted our boys to be little brainiacs. Therefore, we bought the best curriculum for our four-year-old and our upcoming three-year-old as well. We bought the Abeka program with the DVD set and we cannon-balled our way into the deep end of homeschool.

Our normal homeschool days were packed full of watching the teacher on the screen, writing, and reading books. Since I grew up in public school, I was rigid with our schedule. We—or, ahem, *me*, I should say—had a plan and we were going

1

to stick to it. I found myself wanting to have fun, but felt the need to stick to the plan as closely as possible. My pride refused to let me deviate. I had this crazy fear that our kids would fall behind other kids and that drove me to push their little brains too far.

I could tell our kids were antsy and bored at the same time, but that didn't matter. If I'm being honest, I wanted our four-year-old to read and write before all the other kids his age, and I wanted his brother to quickly follow in his footsteps. So, day after day we kept with the same grind, the same plan. Our kids grew miserable. I was miserable. But instead of listening to my inner voice—as well as their cries to change it up some—I pushed more and more.

My misery turned into frustration when our oldest started to struggle writing his ABCs (please don't judge me). I thought to myself, "How hard could this actually be?" I would push, and get frustrated. He would cry, and get upset. Then we both would cry, and become even more unhinged. We went through this cycle for an entire year! I could feel the tension in our relationship, even though he was only four. I told my husband, and myself for that matter, that the kids had to go to "real" school, and I would *never* homeschool again (hint, hint: never say never, my friend). At the time, I simply knew my relationship with my son meant more to me than being his teacher.

The next year we put our oldest in kindergarten. I was so relieved. He seemed better off for it, too. We both seemed less stressed, which made the entire family much happier. However, over the next couple of years of public school things started to become harder and harder for him. His kindergarten, first grade, and second grade teachers all noticed something was off. Our son was struggling in writing and math, and it was starting to take a toll on him.

On the ride home from school, he would say "I am stupid and dumb, and no one likes me." While we did homework at night, he would cry, "I am so stupid and if I can't do it at school, I can't do it at home either." Our happy-go-lucky child was spiraling into a depressed second grader who didn't think he could complete anything on his own. As parents, we were gravely concerned.

Thankfully his second grade teacher (bless her) started to research possibilities for the underlying issue. One day she pulled me aside and explained, "I am not here to diagnose your son, but I have been doing some research, utilizing what I found in class, and it seems to be helping him."

I questioned, "Well, what do you think it is?"

She continued cautiously, "Dysgraphia and dyslexia."

I thank God for that teacher, because if it wasn't for her, we probably would have never thought to get him tested for anything. As parents, it's easy to assume that everything is fine and that your child doesn't need any extra help. After she explained her theory we immediately had him tested outside of the school system. When the results came back exactly as his teacher had suggested they would, we knew we needed to do something—*anything*—to help our son.

The next few months consisted of testing, diagnosing through the school, and talking to them about the kinds of remediations they could put into place for him for the following school year. He took tests through the school and scored high on the reading side, but low on the math side. They whipped those two grades together like flour and eggs in a bowl, and pronounced him "average."

With that interpretation, the administration began telling me our son didn't need any extra help. I quickly explained to them how he would cry and completely crumble during homework sessions, along with reciting the most negative things I had ever heard a second grader confess. The school agreed, "Okay, we can provide limited assistance with a Special Education Teacher once a week, as well as a handful of tweaks to his in-classroom instruction." However, after our meeting, the head of Special Education approached me and admitted: "Mrs. Wasson, unfortunately with the learning disabilities your son has it will be easy for him to fall through the cracks."

Well, I wasn't interested in any part of my son falling through any cracks, but I wasn't sure how to handle the situation if the school wasn't going to help him as I wanted them to, or more importantly, how he needed them to.

The school year ended, and I was at a loss of how to proceed in the months ahead. The stress of solving a problem professional educators could not was too much for me to sit still through, so I tried to forget about the situation and just enjoy the summer with both boys. We would color, play, tell ghost stories during dark and scary thunderstorms, and just enjoy one another's company. One day when we were playing in the backyard, my youngest asked me why we only see lightning when it rains. The question turned into a teaching moment.

During that teaching moment, I heard the Lord whisper in my spirit, *"You are going to homeschool your kids."*

"Excuse me, Lord, pump the breaks," I chuckled and thought to myself. *"Did you not see how all that went down last time? There is no way I am homeschooling my kids."*

"You are going to homeschool your kids," He gently repeated. (Oh, how patient He is with us).

I couldn't believe what I was hearing and feeling deep down in my spirit. I started to panic. "God I cannot do this! I will tell Jeremy when he gets home from work and surely, he will agree I am totally missing what you are saying to me." My husband knew how bad it went last time. I just knew he would be on *my* side.

Friends, I couldn't have been more wrong (insert facepalm here). When Jeremy got home, I told him what I felt the Lord was revealing to me and I could not believe the words that fell from his lips in response, "Well, maybe you need to home-school the kids this year."

I couldn't believe the words coming out of his mouth. He knew how much I was on the struggle bus years before. How could he agree with God? I was distraught. I was upset, unsettled even. I did **I WAS DISTRAUGHT. I WAS UPSET, UNSETTLED EVEN. I DID NOT WANT TO HOMESCHOOL OUR KIDS.** not want to homeschool our kids. I felt ill-equipped. I didn't want to ruin my relationship with our boys. I didn't want to fail *again*.

More than that, I wanted to keep my freedom (say it louder for the people in the back, "Freedom!"). The following year both kids were finally going to be at one school. I was going to have six to seven hours to myself every single day to do whatever I wanted to do. I could write if I wanted to. I could clean, paint, or organize the house if I wanted to. I could get a job and help the family financially if I wanted to. I could finally serve in a ministry if I wanted to. The world was at my fingertips.

However, no matter how much I longed for freedom or added to my mile-long list of excuses as to why I could not homeschool, through the entire summer every time I thought about putting the kids back in school something—or someone, I should say—kept telling me "no." I literally felt as if there was a brick wall stacked in front of me keeping me from doing so. I didn't want to surrender but I knew it was the right thing to do.

Finally, I sheepishly approached my husband and mumbled the words, "I know the Lord is telling me to homeschool our kids. That is what I need to do." While he supported me in the matter, I did not yet support myself. For the next two weeks, I cried. I sobbed like a baby and pitched many toddler fits. I struggled so much with the idea of homeschooling again.

Pulling my weak trust in the Lord and wavering "yes" alongside me, I tried to pack my doubts, insecurities, and excuses into a neat, tiny box where I could not find them, and I reluctantly began putting a plan together for the upcoming school year.

○ ○ ○

Tips for Success #1:
Trust in the Great I AM

Whether your decision to homeschool stemmed from circumstances beyond your control, was a calculated commitment, or a walk of obedience prompted by a gentle whisper from the Holy Spirit, are you in the thick of homeschooling your children and feeling like a crazy person? Maybe you are in your first day of homeschool (or your four-thousandth) and you find yourself feeling just like Moses did when God confronted him about leading the Israelites out of Egypt. Questions and insecurities flood your mind: did I make the right decision? Do I truly have what it takes to homeschool our children? Can I actually lead these kids? Do I really want to continue to give up my freedom?

Can you relate, momma?

I want to encourage you to grab a cup of coffee or tea, take a seat, press the pause button, and take a deep breath. You may feel like you can't do this. I am here to tell you that you *can* do this! God created you to be the mother of your kids. He could have chosen anyone else on the planet, but He chose you! He knew exactly what your kids needed in their life, and He handpicked you and only you for your children.

Likewise, God could have chosen anyone else to help free the Israelites, but He chose Moses. And even in the middle of all of Moses' questions and insecurities, God was patient with him. God even sent him, Aaron. God showed Moses, Aaron, and the Israelites miracles far more spectacular than anything the human imagination could conjure up. He showed them who the *Great I AM* truly is, and that all the universe is at His command.

Momma, if God can command the entire universe into existence and keep it in motion, He can help you homeschool your kids. No, you can't do it on your own, but you can do it armed with the strength that God gives you. And when you forget that fact, God will send you your very own Aaron to hold your arms up and encourage you in your journey. He will bestow miracles beyond what you can imagine to remind you how you were chosen to lead your children.

Yes: you were chosen. You can do this.

God is here to help you. Even if you have a poor attitude. Even if you have a mile-long list of reasons why you can't do it like I did, or even as Moses did, the Great I AM will never leave your side. He will give you the strength you need to keep moving forward.

Prayer:
God, I know that I cannot do this without you. I need you to move, I need you to breathe, and I need you to help me lead these kids. I pray that you help me to surrender my doubts, feelings of insecurities, and fears to you. I pray that in my weakest moments, that you would give me the strength and confidence to keep moving forward. When challenges come, help me to trust in you, the Great I AM.

In Jesus' Name,
Amen

Exodus 3:14, "God replied to Moses, 'I AM WHO I AM.' This is what you are to say to the Israelites: 'I AM has sent me to you.'"

2 Corinthians 12:9, "But he said to me, "My grace is sufficient for you, for my power is made perfect in weakness." Therefore I will boast all the more gladly about my weaknesses, so that Christ's power may rest on me." (NIV)

Let It Out, Girlfriend
(A space to write your thoughts.)

What brought you to homeschool your child/children?
Did you want to homeschool your kids?

_____

_____

_____

_____

_____

_____

_____

_____

_____

_____

_____

_____

_____

Fill Up Your Bookshelf

Momma, you can never have enough resources to pull from on this homeschool journey. Therefore, at the closure of each confession there will be additional resources to encourage you and assist you during this process. To start you out, here are some more scriptures to inspire your soul: Write them down, recite them, learn them, hide them in your heart.

Psalm 34:4, "I sought the LORD, and He answered me and delivered me from all my fears."

Isaiah 41:10, "Do not fear, for I am with you; do not be afraid, for I am your God. I will strengthen you; I will help you; I will hold on to you with My righteous right hand.

Philippians 1:6, "I am sure of this, that He who started a good work in you will carry it on to completion until the day of Christ Jesus." (*in you and your children)

Joshua 1:9, "Haven't I commanded you: be strong and courageous? Do not be afraid or discouraged, for the LORD your God is with you wherever you go."

Proverbs 2:6, "For the LORD gives wisdom; from His mouth come knowledge and understanding."

Isaiah 30:21, "And whenever you turn to the right or to the left, your ears will hear this command behind you: 'This is the way. Walk in it.'"

Galatians 6:9, "So we must not get tired of doing good, for we will reap at the proper time if we don't give up."

Isaiah 43:1-2, "Now this is what the Lord says—the One who created you, Jacob, and the One who formed you, Israel—'Do not fear, for I have redeemed you; I have called you by your name; you are Mine. I will be with you when you pass through the waters, and when you pass through the rivers, they will not overwhelm you. You will not be scorched when you walk through the fire, and the flame will not burn you.'"

Proverbs 31:25-26, "Strength and dignity are her clothing, and she laughs at the time to come. She opens her mouth with wisdom, and the teaching of kindness is on her tongue." (ESV)

Psalm 94:18-19, "If I say, "My foot is slipping," Your faithful love will support me, LORD. When I am filled with cares, Your comfort brings me joy."

John 15:12, "This is My command: Love one another as I have loved you."

1 Peter 5:7, "Cast all your anxiety on him because he cares for you." (NIV)

Psalm 46:10, "He says, "Be still, and know that I am God; I will be exalted among the nations, I will be exalted in the earth." (NIV)

CONFESSION #2

I've Changed Curriculums Multiple Times

When we made our decision to homeschool, it was just a few weeks after wonderful friends of ours also decided to homeschool. We were at a loss as to where to start, so we did what most people do: we emulated what our friends were doing for their family. The program they were using was free. "Free is good," we thought. Plus, we didn't have a lot of time to prepare for the school year, considering I had dragged my feet the entire summer after initially hearing God's voice. So we signed up for the free program online.

Our experience with this particular program was horrendous. Seriously, we all cried every day for the first three weeks. I didn't know how we were going to survive. The problem with the program was it wasn't set up well for our oldest, who was dealing with dysgraphia and dyslexia. Not to mention he was in third grade at this point. For those of you with third graders, I pray for you, because it is one of the hardest years. Students learn an extreme number of new concepts in third grade.

Every day, he hopped online with a teacher for each subject, receiving instructions for forty-five minutes to an hour. Then he had to get back online and read through more information, which took at least forty-five additional minutes for each subject. In addition to that, he had to take a quiz after each lesson that had only five questions. If he got two questions wrong, he automatically failed and couldn't move on until he mastered the test.

After my son took tests three times and still failed, his confidence dropped into the negatives. He already struggled deeply with his confidence and the program wasn't helping at all. He even had paperwork to do on top of the weighty amount of online instruction and quizzes. He was overloaded much like our first years of homeschool—although this time it wasn't directly my doing.

The boys wanted to quit. I wanted to quit. We were all just done, but I felt the need to teach our kids perseverance. I know it may sound silly because they were only in third grade and kindergarten, but for some reason at that moment the lesson was vital. I told the boys, "Listen, I know we are all miserable, but we are going to make the best of it. We are going to finish what we started and do our absolute best to do it with a smile on our faces."

The boys were troopers. I did what I could do to change everything to fit each of our kids' needs so we could finish the school year. I was so proud of them and their tenacity. We didn't always have smiles on our faces, but we finished the school year. We were so ecstatic to be done with the program. I admit we are emotionally scarred from doing this particular online school because any time someone mentions the program's name around us as a family, we cringe.

On top of all of that, our youngest son couldn't help but remember his pre-K year in public school, which had shaped his vision of how school was supposed to be for forever and ever, amen. He thought that school should be nothing but parties and playing outside. I was all for breaks, fun, and doing school all sorts of different ways (I had lightened up a lot since the first attempt at homeschooling), but we had to get him used to sitting some and doing schoolwork. He was not about that life, though.

In pure desperation to make our homeschool days functional and full of joy for the following year, I did my best to build our own curriculum piece by piece, which included attending a co-op every Monday. I hoped by shaking things up a bit and adding a co-op day—along with more field trips—would help our boys to love to learn and grow academically.

I tried to be the finest teacher I could be. I tried to change the way we did things in attempt to discover how each kid learned and tweak things to perfectly fit them, but they still hated school. I was hopeful that piecing together our own curriculum and adding more fun into our days would be the ticket to our kids enjoying homeschooling, but we weren't there yet.

Most of our days, even with my newly crafted ideas, were filled with tears and distaste for school.

To be honest, I felt like I was failing as a homeschool mom. Further, I felt like I was failing them as a mom, period. I was desperate to find something, anything that would help them love school. My husband would cheer me on, "You are doing an excellent job! Stop beating yourself up and keep doing what you are doing! Did you like school when you were a kid?"

"Well, no," I thought to myself.

I knew he was correct, and most kids hate school, but I wasn't satisfied with that because I knew there had to be a better way. I wanted our kids to love to learn.

The same friends whom we followed into the world of internet school saw the frustration on our family's faces one day when we were hanging out. We were worn down and needed a glimmer of hope. We explained to them everything that was going on and they encouraged us, "You have to try Classical Conversations. We let go of our internet days and our kids love it. We have no more tears during our homeschool days." Say what? No more tears sounded heavenly and like a dream; almost too good to be true.

Towards the end of our second year of homeschooling, with a full schedule and a smidgen of hesitancy, we decided to try Classical Conversations. As a mom, I was overwhelmed the first day we went. I felt like I was being waterboarded with information. To my surprise, our kids absolutely loved every single second. While I was in the corner having panic attacks because of all the information being thrown at me, they were soaking it up like sponges and were having the time of their lives. I was so confused. Amid my confusion, I asked God for confirmation, and He washed over me His overwhelming peace. I was convinced we needed to sign up for Classical Conversations as soon as possible.

Other people in our lives thought we were crazy though. Not only because of the ancient model Classical Conversations represents but also because of the number of times we had changed our scholastic rhythm. We had families encouraging us to "just pick something and stick to it." Some argued, "How come one year you made your kids suffer through a program they hated, but now you are so willing to pick up and change what you are doing now?"

I understood where they were coming from because part of me felt the same way. I was ashamed of the plethora of school options we had chosen. Since our oldest had become school-aged, he had gone from three-year-old-school at a church, to pre-K with me, kindergarten at one elementary school, first and second grade at another school, third-grade internet school, and then a concoction of curriculum for fourth grade. As a mom, I knew our kids needed consistency. However, I started to realize that even more than consistency, we needed to find precisely what worked for our family, for our kids.

As I thought about whether we should change things up, something kept coming up in my heart that my oldest brother taught me in my earlier years of being a mom, when I was desperate to find the calling God had on my life. He encouraged me, "Tiffany, the best way to find out what God is calling you to is to do something...*anything*. If you are an anchored ship sitting and doing nothing, you can't be guided by the wind. If you are so anchored and determined to stay where you are in life because *you* know what is best, God can't guide you. He cannot get you to where you need to get to. Lift up your anchor, let God guide you in the direction you are to go."

I didn't know if Classical Conversations was going to fix all our homeschool problems, but I knew that I wanted to keep moving forward and it was obvious what we were doing was not working. I wanted to be guided by The One who has *"His loving eye on me"* (Psalm 32:8, NIV, emphasis mine); better yet, The One who has His loving eyes on our kids. Through the changing and the shifting, I started to realize that God wasn't just guiding me, but also our kids. Our kids are constantly changing daily, weekly, and yearly, and only He knows what is best for them; they are in their own ships with God guiding them.

We have friends who pray every year about homeschooling their kids, putting them in public school, or enrolling them in private school. They are constantly looking to the Father as to how they are to raise *His* kids that He has given them. They realize that their kids are not their own; that they are merely stewards of their lives. Over the years, I have seriously admired this about them. They don't listen to the naysayers who say "pick something and stick to it already." They are constantly looking to His way.

We chose to shift our focus to Classical Conversations, and I am so glad we did! I am so glad we decided not to listen to the skeptics and welcomed something different into our homeschool world. Our kids love Classical Conversations! Has it all been perfect? No. Will we do it until they graduate high school? I don't know yet. I hope so, but at the same time, I don't know who our kids will be in three and five years. They may need

I AM SO GLAD WE DECIDED NOT TO LISTEN TO THE SKEPTICS AND WELCOMED SOMETHING DIFFERENT INTO OUR HOMESCHOOL WORLD.

something totally different by then to become all God has called them to be.

Now, am I saying living flippantly is a way of life? No. We have tried hard to teach our kids to finish what they start. However, we also want to teach our kids to be sensitive to the Holy Spirit. We want them to, "hear a voice behind *them*, saying, '*This* is the way, walk in it,'" and have the confidence to walk in what He is calling them to (Isaiah 30:21, NIV, emphasis added). Sensitivity to the Holy Spirit is something we desperately need to teach children, no matter their age. I don't want our kids to be so hard-pressed to do one thing in their lives that they don't hear God calling them to something different and end up totally missing God's purpose and plan for their lives.

○ ○ ○

Tips for Success #2: Trust the Process

Everything worth building in life takes time: a strong marriage, a ministry, a business. Homeschool is no exception to the rule. When you start homeschooling, it is easy to think everything will automatically fall into place. Now if it does, that is a miracle sister...celebrate! However, for most families, that is the total opposite from the truth that unfolds.

Whenever we started to homeschool, I still had this skewed idea in my perfection-centered mind—even in the middle of my tantrums—that everything was going to be all sunshine, rainbows, and butterflies. I was terribly wrong. We are in our fifth year in a row of homeschooling, and I finally feel like we have created rhythm in our day. We have found a curriculum we love, a schedule that works for us, and the kids wake up most days ready to work and know all that is required of them. However, we did not get here overnight. Our first years of homeschool were filled with tears, sifting through curriculums, and trying to pay real attention to what the Lord was telling us to do.

We had to learn to listen to each other and listen to the Holy Spirit on exactly what was optimal for our *entire* family. We had to learn "when to hold 'em and when to fold 'em," which isn't easy for a stubborn soul like me. The Lord has molded me over the years to be more sensitive to His guidance on how to teach, not just for the sake of who our kids are today, but who they will be in the future; only He knows!

Have you been homeschooling for a while, but right now in your family's homeschool journey everyone is miserable? Are you struggling? Take heart, momma, it will get better. You must give it time; homeschooling is a process. Give yourself time to get to know your kids on a deeper level. Give your kids time to get to know you as their teacher, not just their mom. Do your best not to let everything stress you out, but take it day by day. Also, if everyone is miserable it might be time to try something new. Do not be afraid to try something new; trying something new may be the way for your family to find true happiness and fulfillment in your homeschool days.

If you are a new homeschool mom and you have no idea where to start, just start somewhere. Choose a curriculum and then let God guide you from there. You may end up changing curriculums, which is totally fine. Do not feel like you must have it all figured out on day one! Remember...there is no shame in changing your mind after a while; change doesn't equal failure.

Friends, use every day as an opportunity to listen to the Holy Spirit's instruction on what works best for you and your family. He cares more about you than you can possibly care for yourself. He cares about your kids more than you can possibly ever fathom. Trust Him. Trust the process.

Prayer:
Lord, please help me to be sensitive to what you are calling our family to. You know what is best for all of us. Help us to know which curriculum to use and how to schedule our days. Help us to give homeschooling a chance; to give it time and trust the process. Help us to know when to keep doing what we are doing, and when to let go of our preconceived notions and try something new. Help us to hear your voice above all the other noise. Help us to be still, listen to your voice, and follow you.

In Jesus' Name,
Amen

> Psalm 32:8, "I will instruct you and teach you in the way you should go; I will counsel you with my loving eye on you." (NIV)

> Isaiah 30:21, "Whether you turn to the right or to the left, your ears will hear a voice behind you, saying, 'This is the way; walk in it.'" (NIV)

Free Your Mind

Have you ever changed curriculums? Do you like the curriculum you are currently using? Do you feel like it is time for a change?

_____

_____

_____

_____

_____

_____

_____

_____

_____

_____

_____

_____

Fill Up Your Bookshelf

Here is a list of possible curriculums:

Remember, momma: do not overwhelm yourself by searching through every option in the list below (or through any curriculum for that matter) because the options are endless and can be mind-boggling at times. Also, do not feel limited by the list below; these are just some of the curriculums I am familiar with or have personally tried over the years.

1. Classical Conversations.
2. Abeka.
3. Sonlight.
4. BJU Press.
5. The Good and the Beautiful.
6. Easy Peasy (Free).
7. Create Your Own. (You can piece together things that you find beneficial to your student. You can purchase things from anywhere, however, places such as Barnes and Noble have a homeschool section to help guide you to things you can use for your student, for each subject, and for their current level.)
8. There are public school options online that you can choose from. The public school option we chose did not work for us because it wasn't as flexible as we needed, but they are available. I know people who thrive in the online public school setting.

A very important note:
If you are homeschooling, be sure to investigate your state's requirements for homeschooling. Every state is different. For example, if you are going to homeschool in Georgia, you have to fill out a letter of intent to homeschool your children.

CONFESSION #3

I've Compared Myself to Other Moms

used to play with lizards, make mud pies, and have bleached blond hair tinged with a hint of green from over-swimming in our pool. I was wild and free without a care in the world. I particularly did not care about what others thought of me, nor was I interested in being anyone else. However, as time went on my focus shifted from carefree to careworn. I was less concerned with living and being me and more concerned about being like everyone else.

Now, I am not suggesting I should still be playing with lizards (although some of you might think that would be so cool), or making mud pies, or not treating my hair after a long summer of swimming, but I am suggesting it is important to celebrate who God created me to be. In fact, we all should be celebrating the incredible intricacies and deep individuality bestowed on us by our Creator. Instead, we pick ourselves apart and wonder if we were really meant to be this wondrous, God-breathed creature. I am not sure when this shift happens in life, but unfortunately, it happens to all of us. And once we start it is hard to stop.

Comparison spreads like a cancer, and if we are not careful it can invade every single part of our lives; yes, even our homeschool lives. Homeschool life isn't a dream bubble world where our minds and lives are perfectly protected from everything that used to control us. Homeschool life can be isolating and mentally brutal, magnifying our fleshly short-comings even more. When we sit at home most of our days, it is easy to pick ourselves apart and notice all the things we are not doing for our kids, instead of focusing on our strengths, successes, and all we *are* doing for our kids.

When I started homeschooling our kids, I was a nervous wreck—so throw some comparison fuel on that anxious fire, and I was a hot mess. I was not confident. I wasn't bold in teaching our kids. Everything I did had a question mark at the end of it. Some of this was because I was working through the process of learning how to homeschool, but a lot of it had to do with me looking outside our home at all the other moms to see what they were doing for their kids.

Instead of looking inside our home at exactly what our kids needed, I was Googling everything—or turning to social media to see what we might "need" for homeschool. Looking for ideas? "Go to the internet and find some," It's encouraged. I don't know about you, but the internet and social media can be both a blessing and a curse. You can spend ten minutes getting caught up on all things family, friends, and leave feeling so inspired. Or you can get sucked down the horrendous black hole of comparison.

"Wow, this mom is a writer, blogger, curriculum builder, has her own side business, has a fit fantastic body because she works out every day, seems to get into real clothes and out

of her pajamas every day, and still manages to homeschool her kids. Look at this mom who creates all of these amazingly perfect meals for her family every night; it seems that they never eat the same thing twice." Keeps scrolling. "Now, this mom is a rockstar model, and her children are in advanced stages of learning, excel in sports, and are even learning an instrument on the side."

I don't know about you, but when I get caught up in looking at all of these other fantastic moms, I start to berate myself with questions such as, "What on earth am I doing wrong? Why can't I be more like them? If I could be more like them, then our homeschool life, our entire lives, would be better."

When we made our home with Classical Conversations, I was so excited about the community because I hoped I would finally be able to get outside of the home, out of my own head, and focus on something else...anything else.

But let's be real: Does anyone honestly think you can take someone who habitually compares themselves to others, put them in a room with ten remarkable homeschool moms, and that the differences won't be amplified in their mind?

I remember the first day I stepped into the church where we met for Classical Conversations; that day I learned every single person there was a phenomenal homeschool parent. They were smart, innovative, and seemed to know who they were and all their kids needed. I was intimidated. I was so jealous of them. I wanted to be them.

Thankfully, some of the women in the community read my mail almost immediately and lovingly pointed me in the right direction. One day I openly confessed to one of the other moms, "I wish I was more like you. You are such an amazing homeschool mom." She encouraged, "Tiffany, so are you, stop being so hard on yourself. Stop trying to be like everyone else; be you. That is who your kids need." I was shocked at her answer and thought, *"Wait, what? You are giving me permission to be myself. Now, that is a novel idea."*

I could finally take a deep breath.

For the first time in our homeschool journey, for the first time in a long time, I felt at peace with myself. I felt calm. I was able to start thinking more clearly and start to dissect and establish who I was, who God created me to be. I was able to ask myself the question, "Who is Tiffany?" and feel the freedom to answer with the whole truth and nothing but the truth. I must confess that finding the truth has been extremely enlightening, to say the least.

I have learned I am not a Pinterest mom.

One day the kids and I decided to make chocolate chip banana muffins. We read the recipe, got out all the right ingredients, and went to town making this yummy breakfast delight. We measured, poured, and waited patiently for them to rise in the oven. The muffins were ready, and we could not wait to eat them. We put one on a plate for everyone, got a cold glass of almond milk, and each took an enormous bite.

As quick as the muffins went into our mouths, the bite we took ended back onto the plate. My oldest shouted, "These taste like sanitizer!" My youngest followed, "These are awful!" I agreed with both of them. I grabbed the recipe printout and scoured it to see where we went wrong and we had put baking soda instead of baking powder, and salt instead of sugar. "Well, we had a blast making them, right boys?" Although we were disappointed we didn't get to eat the muffins, we all agreed the process was enjoyable and laughed hysterically at our mishap.

I am not the one to find all the arts, crafts, and desserts that I possibly can and make them perfectly for my kids. I am the mom who prepares their hearts and minds for a "Pinterest fail" when I make something with my kids. I have taught my kids that the fun we have making something, such as a yummy dessert, matters more than looking flawless in the end. If we had a blast making it or if it tastes good, we have won!

I have learned I liked to be organized.

Organization in our home gives me so much tranquility. When things are in disarray and there is clutter everywhere, my brain cannot function properly. Since I like to be organized, I have found that the laminator, folders, crates, and cubbies are all my best friends. Everyone in the house also has their own space to keep their things together and at the end of the day, I want everything we have gotten out for the day to go back where it belongs, back to its home. I have a hard time walking into Tuesday if Monday is still scattered all over the living room floor and dining room table. Sometimes my obsessiveness with having clean, organized workspaces drives the rest of my family insane, but they have learned that it helps me to function so most of the time they do a sensational job giving into my craziness

I have learned having a schedule is vital to the heartbeat of our days.

For a couple of years, I felt like having a schedule was stressful because I hated being put under time constraints (yes, I am that girl who is always late), but I finally realized we need something to guide us and help us get everything done in a timely manner. We don't always stick to the schedule to a "T," but we try and it has helped us a lot. I also work better with a lesson plan. Some moms do not like to have a lesson plan, but I have learned it helps us so much. Our lives function better with a calendar and lesson plans close by our sides.

I have learned everyone has different capacities in life. (The biggest lesson I have learned as of late.)

I used to think I had to fill up my plate with the same things everyone else was doing in their lives. I would see a mom on social media whose bio read "Author of five cookbooks. Family blogger. Fitness fanatic. Homeschool momma to 5. Lover of Louis Vuitton and my freshly planted garden," and thought I had to do all the things she did or have all that she had to be successful (or happy even).

A friend of mine recently pointed out to me everyone has different capacities in life. She lovingly reassured, "A mom who has an at-home business wakes up early in the morning to work on her business because that fills her. You wake up early to write because that is what fills you, which is a beautiful thing. Not everyone has to fill their plates with the same things in life, or even the same amount. Everyone has different capacities, and it is foolish to try to carry the load that was meant for someone else to carry." Just wow!

In the past few years, I have learned so much about myself while being a part of our homeschool community. I have truly been able to lean into who God has created me to be and celebrate that person. I have also been able to look at other people, see who God has created them to be, and celebrate them and their strengths.

I see my friend Adrienne, who is even more organized than I am with all her binders for every part of her family's life, and I can celebrate that now. I am so happy for her. Instead of giving her the cut-eye of jealousy (seriously, I shamefully did this). I

IN THE PAST FEW YEARS, I HAVE LEARNED SO MUCH ABOUT MYSELF WHILE BEING A PART OF OUR HOMESCHOOL COMMUNITY.

can look at my friend Britney, who sometimes changes her family's homeschool schedule monthly, and express, "That sounds like it would be stressful to me, but it works for your family and that is amazing." I can now look at the mom on social media, the very one who is doing *all the things,* and admit I have no idea how she does it all, but encourage, "More power to you girlfriend, you rock on with your bad self."

I am so thankful for community because I do believe if it wasn't for it, I would not be who I am today. Since fully embracing community, I love myself and others more than I ever have before. Furthermore, our lives have been so much more beautiful and a lot less stressful since adding it to our lives.

○ ○ ○

Tips for Success #3:
Embrace Community

Not even Jesus did life alone, so I do not know why we think we can isolate ourselves and be successful at anything in our lives. Community is vital for survival, encouragement, and growth.

Homeschooling without other people in your life is possible, but I promise you, burnout isn't far away if you try—along with discouragement, comparison, and the constant thoughts of wanting to quit when it gets hard. Before I embraced community with others I was lost, trying to be something I wasn't, and to be honest, I was downright frightened. I was terrified I was going to ruin myself or my kids in the process of home-schooling them.

The parents I have done life with over the past few years have helped me grow in confidence and have been there to help me discover who I truly am as a person. They have helped me to celebrate my abilities, have given me people to relate to, and have gently shown me necessary areas of growth and how to obtain it. They have also motivated me to keep on going when I want to quit homeschooling our kids—and sometimes this has been on the daily.

My advice is if you are not in a homeschool community, get into one as soon as possible. Again, you can be successful without one, but it helps so much! Not only will you be better off for it, but your kids will also be better off for it as well.

Furthermore, just as much as it is necessary to be a part of a community, you must be sure you are in the right one. Homeschool community should be a place of encouragement; a place to receive and give encouragement. When you go to a community, it should be a breath of fresh air; a place where you can be refreshed and restored.

You should be challenged to grow. Having people accept you for who you are doesn't mean that they do not challenge you to grow. There are always areas where you can improve. It's too easy to become complacent and accepting of the current version of who you are, thinking "I am who I am, and I am never going to change." That is a dangerous place to be; we are called to be people who are lifelong learners and who are constantly striving towards growth.

A community should also be a place filled with compassion. There have been many days where I came ill-prepared to teach something and grace was given. We are all families with full schedules, and we understand that life can happen. On the days when I have messed up or fallen short and feel awful, the people in my homeschool group help me to brush it off, fill in the gaps, and help me to smile again.

Can community be a place of frustration? Absolutely. They are filled with people and people can be frustrating at times. But if you are in a place where there is constant judgment, guilt, lack of help, lack of empathy, self-centeredness, and belittlement...you may want to look for another place.

The disciples were a difficult group of men to deal with, but Jesus still led them with love, compassion, and gentle correction. I don't know about you but that is the type of community I want to be a part of.

Prayer:
Lord, I know it isn't healthy or smart to do life alone. I know I need people in my life. I know my kids need people in their lives. I ask that not only will you help our family find a community, but I pray you help us to find the right community. I don't want a community just for the sake of having one, but I want one so each person in our family can learn, be encouraged, and grow into who you created us to be. Please lead us in the right direction. Please lead us to people who want to be more like Jesus and encourage us to do the same.

In Jesus' Name,
Amen

> John 13:15, "For I have given you an example, that you also should do just as I have done to you."

Tell Me About It

How have you compared yourself to other moms? How did you overcome it? What truth did you learn about yourself or them? How will you use community to avoid this pitfall in the future?

_____

_____

_____

_____

_____

_____

_____

_____

_____

_____

_____

_____

_____

Fill Up Your Bookshelf

How to find community:

1. Classical Conversations: When you join Classical Conversations there is a place online on their website that helps you to find a community closest to you, which can be extremely helpful.

2. Church: If you are plugged into the local church, simply asking if there are other homeschool families who attend your church can open a whole world of opportunities and guidance for you. You might be surprised to find that there are a lot of others just like you, which can give you instant community.

3. Facebook: Facebook is an amazing tool to help you on your homeschool journey. You can type in "homeschool groups in my area" in the search bar and a lot of options will show up for you.

4. Google: Google is a very helpful tool as well, which may be a given, but I just wanted to remind you. If you type in "homeschool communities near me" you will find something there for you and your family.

* Remember, do not fall into the pit of comparison.

CONFESSION #4

I've Compared Our Kids to Other Kids

I sank deeper into the park bench as a new friend of mine—a seasoned homeschool mom—kept talking to me about her children. She went on and on about all they could do at their ages; some things were above their age requirements, and some were spot on. I was excited for her and her intelligent children, however, the more she spoke the more I felt like my children were subpar. I had this enormous growth of inadequacy take over the pit of my stomach. Questions started to haunt my brain: are my kids behind? Where do they *need* to be? What can I do to get them there? What can I do to make them excel above where they are "supposed" to be in their education?

These questions not only started to haunt me, but they drove me to "crack the whip," so to speak, when it came to our homeschool days. I tried to add more and more work to our days, which didn't challenge our children but overworked them. I tried to teach them the way other moms taught their kids, which wasn't necessarily the way my children learned best. I would push our children without a clear reason or purpose to this unclear, moving finish line they could never reach. I would push until frustration rushed through their brains and tears ran down their faces.

Then, I would catch myself during playdates starting to brag about where my kids were and all they were excelling at in school, when deep down I knew we were all miserable, especially them. But knowing my kids were "learning" and "growing," I was fine with the way I was treating my children.

However, one day as I watched tears roll down our oldest son's face, I was awakened to the fact I was pushing way too hard, and my eyes were opened to the damage I was causing our kids. After this awakening, the Holy Spirit prompted, *"Tiffany, are you trying to make your children better, or are you trying to make yourself look better?"* Ouch!

The homeschool life, if not handled with care, can become a major competition in which our children become the trophy. I am not sure why this happens. Perhaps since we are homeschooling parents and stuck at home all the time, we feel a lack of accomplishment, so our children become our accomplishment. We feel as if we aren't doing anything ourselves, and therefore, our children become our focus and our prize; something we can show off to others so that they can see how remarkable we are.

> **THE HOMESCHOOL LIFE, IF NOT HANDLED WITH CARE, CAN BECOME A MAJOR COMPETITION IN WHICH OUR CHILDREN BECOME THE TROPHY.**

Not only is this such a selfish way to live, but our children do not become better off because of it. This way of living and acting doesn't encourage our kids, it does the total opposite.

Any confidence we thought they had, is quickly torn down by the words we pronounce to others. We may think they aren't listening, but they are.

"My kid is in 5th grade and is reading at an 8th-grade level."

"If my child stays on the current path he is on, he will certainly finish his associates degree before he is out of high school."

"Well, my kid knows all of his multiplication facts and he is only in second grade."

"My youngest can write better than my oldest and he is only in third grade."

"My youngest is going to be a genius at math, he does it so quickly and so accurately already."

How do I know beyond any doubt that our children are listening? Because I have heard it in their self-deprecating speech. I have heard my oldest articulate, "If my younger brother is so great at math then he should just skip a grade or even do the math I am doing."

My youngest has voiced things such as, "I can't write creatively like my brother. He is older and better than me. I will never be as good as him."

Yes, sometimes they have said things they have come up with on their own, or they have even skewed things I have said. But for the most part, the ways in which they compare themselves to each other are things that have *literally* come out of my mouth. Their lack of confidence has somewhat been my fault. By realizing this, I have been able to do some major backtracking and remind myself and our children of major truths in order to help get us back on track and rebuild our kids' confidence.

Truth #1: Our kids do not learn like every other kid.

Every single person in the universe is different. How do I know this fact? Through something as simple as the finger-print. No two people have the same grooves on their hands... not even twins. If something as simple as the fingerprint makes us unique, I am not sure how we expect something as complex as our brains to work the same.

I learned that both of our kids have unique needs once I got them both tested. As explained earlier, we found that our oldest has dysgraphia and dyslexia. Later we found that he also has processing speed struggles. We got our youngest tested as well and found out that he has sensory and auditory processing struggles. After I got them tested, I did a ton of research to help myself to learn different ways to teach their individual needs.

I started homeschooling, well, because God told me to. But once we continued the process, I started to grasp the major benefits. The biggest payoff is the fact I don't have to shove our kids into this rigid way of learning; we have the space to help our kids to discover how they learn and thrive. Public schools have their challenges, and one of them is that when there is a classroom of twenty-five or more kids, it is hard to meet the distinct needs of every child. The beauty of home-schooling is I get a lot of one-on-one time with my children to help them in exactly the way they receive help.

It has also been so liberating to discover that instead of being forced to mold our kids to a curriculum, I am free to mold a curriculum to fit the needs of our kids. For example, if our oldest needs more time in math or doesn't understand something, we can slow down and really focus on exactly what he is struggling with; we have the time to make sure that he understands a concept before moving on. Sometimes my internal public school mind freaks out about this, and I regress back to, "We have to be at a certain place in the book at a certain time," but I do my best to hush those urges and work with our kids. Time and curriculums do not have to work against us, they can work in our favor.

Truth #2: I do not homeschool our kids so they can be like everyone else.

When I was in school there were so many outside influences it was hard for me to truly discover who I really was or who God created me to be. The beauty of homeschooling is most of the outside influences do not exist, so it is easier for kids to realize who they are, and we get the opportunity to guide them to this truth. I love that I get to speak into our kids' lives daily and remind them they are not like everyone else and that is a good thing.

Our oldest is super creative. He loves to build things. His room is full of Legos, and it has been since he was three. His love for building has done some major damage to the bottom of my feet over the years (yay Legos!) but the creations he builds blow my mind. I love to watch him create. However, a love for building and creating comes paired with a love for taking things apart; obviously, this drives me bonkers sometimes. He often likes to take things apart that do not belong to him and then doesn't know how to put them back together, so dad must step in.

But through all of this construction and demolition, I have grown sensitive to the fact that he has an architectural mind and sees things differently than anyone else sees them, even if he struggles academically sometimes. Does he sometimes write numbers backward? Yes. Does he have issues getting his creative ideas on paper? Yes. However, when he struggles, I remind him his penmanship will develop gradually, but in the meantime, we celebrate the creative ideas he does have. Seriously, he comes up with some astonishing ideas!

Furthermore, I get to remind him that his brain is awe-inspiring. I remind him writing things backward is something he needs to work on correcting, but it is so cool his brain does what it does; it simply means his brain interprets things differently than everyone else. Someday this will be used by God in his favor. A time will come when everyone he works with will see a task one way, and he will be fully equipped to bring an entirely different concept to the table. His ability to create, to see things differently than anyone else will help him so much in his life. Who knows, with his outside-of-the-box thinking, he may even change the world one day.

Our youngest is full of joy, energy, thinks on the go, and is constantly singing his heart out. Most of the time it sounds like a herd of elephants in our house because of our youngest. He is constantly jumping up and down, and in between jumps he is calculating math, reading, and writing to the best of his abilities. I thought his energy level would keep him from learning, and sometimes it does, but for the most part he is impeccable at focusing on what is important when it is important, completing it, and then of course he gets back to moving.

Yes, sometimes this drives me insane. I just want to hold his shoulders, stare into his eyes, and beg him to be still and quiet. He is static for a moment, a very short moment, and then off he goes on another adventure. Although most of the time I want to pin him down to his desk (and yes, we do work with him on his ability to be still because it's important to be able to do that) we celebrate his ability to learn on the go.

Is our house quiet? Not at all! But it is full of song, laughter, and joy. I see his ability to learn while staying on his toes as a major asset in his life. He will be tenacious and do everything with a smile on his face. He will use his gift to encourage others to persevere with a smile on their faces. Sure, maybe he'll be a performer or entertainer in the future, only God knows. However, I know that whatever he does he will be successful and a forceful, positive influence for change.

Truth #3: They are still kids.

One of my biggest downfalls is I am constantly looking towards the future. One of my dear friends, Elizabeth, pointed this out to me as we were talking one day about our kids and where they were academically. My speech started to frantically spiral out of control: "Right now our seventh grader is struggling with fractions. I am kind of worried because if he doesn't get it now, then he is going to struggle when he is in high school. If he struggles in high school, then he is going to struggle when he is in college. If he struggles in college then he won't be able to get a job and support his family." Yes, I went there.

"You aren't there yet," she gently reminded me. (Thank you, Elizabeth!)

"Wait, what?"

"I have found myself worrying about where my kids will be as well," she continued, "But I have to constantly remind myself that we aren't there yet and to focus on today."

Oftentimes I put so much pressure on my kids for who they will become, rather than focusing on who and where they are right now. Do I want my child to understand fractions? Yes. But should my push for him to learn fractions be fueled by my vision of where he should be in six years, or from where he is now? The two places are so different. Meeting my son right in the middle of his current struggle is a lot less intense than approaching him from a place of worry about where he will be in six years.

When I connect with him with today in mind, I am a lot more patient, understanding, and gentle. When I swoop down from my post of unreasonable anxiety, I am more irritable, less patient, and even angry sometimes, none of which produce a positive response or understanding from our son.

When we as parents create a learning environment full of fear, worry, and panic, the pressure can cause our children to snap and even grow to hate learning. Furthermore, the things we try to teach them most likely won't stick. However, when we create an environment of love, understanding, and encouragement, real authentic learning can happen. In return, the things we teach them will become embedded and they may even one day love to learn.

○ ○ ○

Tips for Success #4:
Love Them Where They Are Now

God is so patient with us. He doesn't look at us and scoff, "I will love you when you have completely eliminated that sin, when you never struggle with fear again, or when you reach the pinnacle of everything I know you will become. Then I will love you; then I will be patient with you." He loves us right where we are. Does He want us to grow? Yes. He doesn't want us to stay in our sin, to keep struggling with the same fears, or never reach our full potential. But He also doesn't bully us into repentance or into forced transformation. He doesn't helicopter around, waiting for us to flounder so He can call us out on it and point out the particulars of how we messed up. Instead, He patiently and lovingly nudges us toward benchmarks of change and personal growth.

My children—your children—need the same. They need us to lovingly and patiently help them grow. They need us to focus on who they are now and their current struggles, not who they will be and what they might struggle with ten years from now. As both teachers and students, we need to be reminded that they aren't like everyone else and they don't learn like everyone else, and that's okay. They are uniquely created individuals fashioned by a complex God, and that is something we should help them internalize.

Prayer:
Lord, please help me celebrate the children you have created and given to me exactly as you made them, instead of comparing them to every other person. They are your

creations, your children, so please help me to treat them as such. Help me to lovingly guide them to grow; to teach them with patience. You treat me with mercy, grace, and steadfast love; help me to treat them the same. Teach me to celebrate their strengths and gently guide them through their weaknesses. You are the ultimate Teacher. Please Lord, help me to continue to learn from you.

In Jesus' Name,
Amen

> Psalm 103:8, "The LORD is merciful and gracious, slow to anger and abounding in steadfast love. (ESV)

> Proverbs 18:21, "Life and death are in the power of the tongue, and those who love it will eat its fruit."

Don't Hold Back

How have you compared your kids to other kids? How did it make your kids feel? How do you think you can make things right with your child/children after they have noticed the comparison/comparisons? What can you do moving forward to ensure you celebrate them instead of making them feel inadequate?

_____

_____

_____

_____

_____

_____

_____

_____

_____

_____

_____

_____

_____

Fill Up Your Bookshelf

Remember your opinion of your children means the most to them. You are their mom. You have the power to lift them up or tear them down; as the Bible says, to bring life or death. Pay close attention to the words you speak. Here is a list of positive affirmations to proclaim over your children:

1. You are so smart.
2. You are loved.
3. You are not alone.
4. You're a treasure.
5. You make my life better.
6. I am so thankful for you.
7. You mean the world to me.
8. You are so beautiful/handsome.
9. You were created on purpose for a purpose.
10. Everyone makes mistakes.
11. Your grades do not define who you are.
12. You will be successful.
13. You are unique.
14. I love ____ about you.
15. Thank you for trying your best.
16. You taught me something new today.
17. God's got this.
18. Keep your head up.
19. Strive for quality, not quantity (This is one of our homeschool mottos).
20. Strive for progress, not perfection (Another one of our homeschool mottos).

CONFESSION #5

I Don't Always Respond the Right Way

There is something inside of me that expects everything to be perfect. I don't know why; I know perfection cannot be fully attained until we get to heaven. However, day in and day out I expect everything to be completely in line, like rows of well-trained soldiers. I wake up in the morning and just know that my two handsome boys are going to slide out of their comfy beds and emerge like complete angels. They are going to respond to their sibling out of love, they are going to be excited to learn and do their schoolwork, and they are going to do all their chores without any complaints.

And every mom shouts, "Yeah right!"

I know nothing will ever be flawless—especially in a home with four people who are completely different. But that doesn't stop me from expecting perfection will be my reality. So when it isn't, it is like a switch flips and I tend to state things I cannot take back. The kind of things that make you want to crawl into a hole and just die.

Things such as...

"Come on, why are you dragging your feet, we've got to get started. We need to get our Bible reading over and done with, so we get to our actual school stuff."

"Why are you still doing math; it is taking you entirely too long. We can't spend this long doing math, dude, we have other subjects to get to."

"Why did you call your brother stupid, would you like it if I called you stupid?"

"What are you thinking? You should know this by now, we have gone over this for like three days."

"This is, like, the third year you have been doing this; can we just learn it already and move on?"

"Bro, you are stressing me out right now; I just can't deal with you."

Shamefully, I have vocalized *every single one of these things*. Whenever I have let my flesh take over and allow my mouth to throw fiery darts, the look on my kid's face makes my heart feel sick.

In those moments I know I have disappointed them. I know they hate the idea that they have disappointed me. I know I've crushed any kind of confidence they may have had to keep moving forward. I know I have weighed them down with a ton of bricks in the form of heavy words.

Furthermore, when I utter things I shouldn't say, I see their somber faces and I am not quick to confess I am sorry.

Sometimes my face represents an attitude of, *"Yeah, I said it, whatcha going to do about it?"* It's as if I hate to admit I have failed them in any way. I don't want them to see my imperfections. So, I pretend I don't have any and they just have to accept what I profess as I walk away.

Then the Holy Spirit speaks, *"Tiffany you are being a bully."*

"Um, what? No, I am not, Holy Spirit. They just need to be better, do better, and do what I say. They are just being disrespectful, disobedient, and lazy."

"Tiffany, you are being ugly, go and apologize to your kids."

"I can't do that Lord, then they will see that I have weaknesses."

"Exactly."

Weakness is something we do not like to admit that we have, especially to our children. We desire them to think we have it all

> WEAKNESS IS SOMETHING WE DO NOT LIKE TO ADMIT THAT WE HAVE, ESPECIALLY TO OUR CHILDREN.

together. We think if we show any kind of weakness or fault, they will use it against us. However, one of the best things we can do for our children is to admit to them we are not perfect. We need to show them true humility by asking for forgiveness and showing them true repentance and real life-change.

If we never show our kids what this process looks like, they will never be able to admit when they are wrong. They will never know how to ask for forgiveness; they will never know what it looks like to truly repent. Not to mention, if our children walk around with parents who put themselves on a pedestal and constantly kick others down, then they too will grow up with a high and mighty mindset and think they are better than everyone else and do not need to grow in any way.

Pride will be their warm blanket. Pride will be their way of life, which will keep them in a hamster wheel of blaming others throughout their life for everything wrong in their life. They will ultimately never take responsibility for anything they have done; it will always be someone else's fault.

I got to a point where I not only realized a lot of the words I was verbalizing to our kids were extremely wrong, but I also wanted more for our kids. I wanted them to be able to admit when they were wrong. I wanted them to be able to humble themselves and ask for forgiveness. I wanted them to see me struggle so they would know they are not the only ones who struggle. I wanted to be real with my children.

The first time I apologized to my oldest for something, I admitted I was wrong; it felt extremely unnatural, like a duck walking backward. I sat down in a chair so I could be at his level, stared into his bold green eyes, and hesitantly allowed the words to roll off of my tongue.

"Buddy, I am so sorry I said ugly things to you. I should have never said that to you. You didn't deserve the way I treated you. Sometimes Mommy gets stressed and says things she should never say. Homeschooling isn't always easy for me either. I worry sometimes if I am doing enough for you to help you be where you need to be. I let worry and fear get in the way. I let my worry and fear get the best of me and I say things to hurt you, so I am not the only one who is worried, fearful, or hurting. I am so sorry. Can you please forgive me?"

Wow! I wish that I would have taken a picture of the look on his face. He had so much relief on his face. The weight I had piled on with words was lifted off. He could breathe again. I could breathe again.

My son finally understood where I was coming from; the reason I was acting out. He realized I get stressed too. He realized that fear and worry can take over me as well, even as a parent. He realized I am not just a mommy-robot with calculated responses. He realized I am a human with real emotions which are sometimes followed by sinful responses.

My apology opened up a new level of communication I'd never enjoyed with my son before, and eventually with both of my sons. Over time, vulnerability has become our norm. We have been able to share with each other how we are feeling; on our good days and bad days. My oldest son shares with me when not only math is a struggle but when he is just having an awful day or isn't "feeling" school that day. We all have off days, don't we? But for some reason, we don't believe that bad days happen for kids. We expect them to be happy-go-lucky all of the time and never have a bad case of the Mondays.

As a family, instead of succumbing to the overwhelming pressure to barrel blindly through our to-do lists, we can finally be open and honest with each other. We can disclose, "You know, I am just not feeling it today." And that's perfectly okay. (But we are still going to get our school done, can I get an amen?!). I can now reassure our kids that on some days they aren't going to want to do anything, and that is normal. But even when we as humans feel that way, we still have to press through and get the job done.

Now, instead of me walking around with a "fe, fi, fo, fum" attitude, we can all enjoy each other's company, do our best to persevere through a bad case of the Mondays, and try to make each other laugh—to make our hard work fun amidst the craziness. Confessing to our boys I am not perfect and asking for forgiveness has been a life-changer for sure, but that is not where it ends.

It isn't enough for me to just confess to our boys when I mess up and ask for forgiveness; it is vital to show them true repentance. If I apologize because I spoke something out of turn but then I continue to allow my tongue to inflict damage, not only am I not being fair to them, but I am also not helping them grow at all. And I am especially not helping myself. They need to see I am striving to do better in my weakest areas.

They also need to hear me asking for God to help me. They need to know exactly where true strength comes from. None of us can get better on our own. We need God's help, and we need the help of those around us; even more so when it is a sin we struggle with daily.

My boys and I have prayed together over so many areas of our lives we struggle with. We have prayed for mommy to be able to let go of perfectionism. We have prayed mommy can speak out of love and not anger. We have prayed mommy can have joy in her heart and not frustration. We have prayed our youngest will learn how to deal with his rage in a healthy way (we are all hotheaded people apparently). We have prayed our youngest would love to read. We have prayed our oldest would have a better attitude towards others. We have prayed he would not hate math (he treats math like it is going to come off the pages and punch him; he gets so irritated at it).

After we have prayed for certain areas in our lives, we have agreed to hold each other accountable. Now when we say or do things we have promised we wouldn't anymore, we gently remind each other and love each other through it. For instance, when I have spoken things I promised I wouldn't express any more, our boys gently remind me, "But mommy, you said you wouldn't say that anymore."

"Boys you are absolutely right! Thank you for reminding me."

We have prayed for so many areas of our lives. We have also held each other accountable for so many things we have prayed for. Are we perfect? No. But we are on the road to sanctification together and I wouldn't have it any other way.

○ ○ ○

Tips For Success #5: Let Them See You Fail

Moms, when you homeschool you are around your children a lot! They are going to see the good and the bad and the ugly that is in you. You are going to see the good and the bad and the ugly that is in them. It is vital for your home that you create an atmosphere of true confession, forgiveness, and repentance.

Say it with me, "Confession. Forgiveness. Repentance."

It is not enough to confess you are sorry. Just uttering words won't do any good if there isn't any real change behind the words. If you just claim you are sorry and ask for forgiveness and never change, your kids will eventually not trust the words you speak. They are going to think to themselves, "Well, mommy is going to say she is sorry, but she doesn't really mean it."

Friend, I am not saying you will never mess up again after you voice you are sorry, but your kids need to see real progress in the areas you struggle with.

Progress. Not perfection.

Repeat it with me: "progress, not perfection." I am not implying you have to be perfect for your children. I am just saying you need to be real with yourself and with them. Let it be known you are struggling, but also let it be known you are asking God for help on a daily basis and for Him to help you grow and thrive. Your children will be better off for it, and of course so will you!

Prayer:
Lord, please help our family to develop an atmosphere of true confession, forgiveness, and repentance in our home. Help us to be honest with you and each other when we are having a horrible day or when we are struggling with habitual sin. Help us to ask for forgiveness and forgive quickly; to show grace upon grace. Help us and give us the strength to repent and change for the better. Please forgive us for all the times when we have been stubborn and didn't want to change, and please forgive us when we will struggle with this exact thing in the future. Lord, we know we are human, and we are going to mess up but help us to strive to be more like you. We love you!

In Jesus' Name,
Amen

2 Corinthians 7:9, "Now I rejoice, not that you were made sorry, but that your sorrow led to repentance. For you were made sorry in a godly manner, that you might suffer loss from us in nothing." (NKJV)

Proverbs 28:13, "The one who conceals his sins will not prosper, but whoever confesses and renounces them will find mercy."

John 1:16-17, "Indeed, we have all received grace after grace from His fullness, for the law was given through Moses, grace and truth came through Jesus Christ."

Confess It, Girl

What are some of the negative comments you have spoken to your children? Have you modeled true confession, forgiveness (asking and giving), and repentance in your home? If not, how can you take the first step and start today?

_____

_____

_____

_____

_____

_____

_____

_____

_____

_____

_____

_____

_____

Fill Up Your Bookshelf

Forgive yourself, momma.

Momma, I am here to encourage you to forgive yourself. As moms, we tend to beat ourselves up so much. Even if we confess, ask for forgiveness, and repent, we still beat ourselves up; trapping ourselves in a vicious cycle of thoughts on how we could have handled a situation better. We hold ourselves to such high standards and make ourselves feel like we are never supposed to mess up. We are not God, we are human. We are going to mess up!

You have to learn to give yourself grace just as you would any other person...just as you give to your children. Not only is it important to teach your children how to forgive others, but you also have to teach them to forgive themselves, by way of example, to truly accept the grace in which God freely gives. Grace isn't something we earn; it is something we have to accept. Grace is a gift. Teach your children how to accept it and continue growing by accepting it yourself; by refusing to bury yourself in guilt, shame, and regret.

CONFESSION #6

There Are Days I Want to Quit

My youngest wouldn't stop crying about writing in his journal. I don't mean little tears here-and-again-crying, I mean crocodile tears and sure panic-along-with-it kind of crying. I wasn't asking him to do anything he had not done before. He was just refusing to do it. He said it was "too hard", but I had a journal full of words made into sentences which proved to me otherwise.

"Buddy, this isn't anything you haven't done before. You can do this, I promise. Just write and be done with this." He took a deep breath and proceeded to cry.

"You have to stop." He wouldn't. I could have tried spanking him, which I have tried in the past, but this kid doesn't respond well to that kind of discipline all the time. I could tell this was going to be one of those times. It wasn't about whether or not he was going to write in his journal anymore, it became a battle of who could stick it out the longest. (We are both the stubborn kind).

I tried to keep my cool, but his crying was beating and wearing down my door of patience.

"If you don't stop crying, I am taking your tablet away and you are grounded." He didn't stop crying, so the tablet was mine. Of course, taking away his tablet made him cry even more. The crying was like nails on a chalkboard. I was spent. I was done. I was boiling. I felt like a cartoon character burning with anger, red in the face, and about to explode.

"That's it, I quit! Everyone is going on that yellow school bus tomorrow! Go put your face in the corner, I am done!" I stomped off as our son cried himself to sleep in the corner, wrapped up in a blanket; he slept for two hours. Maybe he just needed a nap. Maybe he was just being stubborn and was trying to find a way to wriggle out of his work. Regardless of what was wrong with him, shamefully, this was not my finest moment. Especially since I had promised our boys I would quit threatening that I was going to put them back in school every time homeschool was hard.

> "THAT'S IT, I QUIT! EVERYONE IS GOING ON *THAT* YELLOW SCHOOL BUS TOMORROW! GO PUT YOUR FACE IN THE CORNER, I AM DONE!"

I tried to excuse my behavior, but I knew it was wrong. I do not think the way my son was acting was right either, but I was the adult in the room, and I knew better. After our son woke up, I apologized for what I said to him. Then we had a long conversation about his behavior and how it was unacceptable. We hugged it out and our day got better...until reading time, that is.

Another time where I lost my cool (and there have been many times, my friend) was one day when our oldest was taking forever to do his math. I mean forever. I think it was close to three hours he spent doing one math lesson. Now, I know I probably should have not let him sit there for that long, but it was another one of those situations where I was trying to be an immovable force.

He started out the day not wanting to do math. Really, what kid wants to do math first thing in the morning? But if we don't do it first thing, he really struggles later in the day with it. This particular morning, I tried to shake him out of his attitude and failed. I taught him his new lesson, circled problems, and went on my merry way. I tried to do dishes, laundry, check on our youngest and make sure he was doing his school, and see if he needed any help. I kid you not, when I say that every single time I looked at our oldest he was doing everything but doing his math, I mean every single time.

I would fold a shirt, look up, and he was staring off into the distance.

"Dude, do your math."

"Yes, ma'am."

I would fold another garment, look up, and he was playing with his pencil.

"Do your math!"

"Okay." He grabbed his pencil the right way and proceeded to try to do his work.

I finished the laundry and moved on to the dishes. I looked up and he was drawing characters on his paper.

"I am going to go crazy, son. Focus on your math."

"I will."

Yes, this went on for three hours! And once the three hours were up, I checked his math and he got most of them wrong. Wrong!

"Bro, what are you doing today? I quit! I cannot do this anymore. I am done!"

Homeschool is not for the faint of heart. Some days are fantastic, and it is easy to get caught up in all the ways that homeschool is ideal. Then other days you want to pull your hair out, scream at everybody, and shout to everyone you know all the ways homeschool was a terrible idea and you wished you never did it.

Homeschool is hard and it tests every portion of your mind, body, and spirit.

There have been so many days I have wanted to call it quits. Some days are because of the way the kids react to not wanting to do things. Other days are because I want to tap out and let someone else take over and give them the responsibility of educating my children. However, a lot of times I have wanted to quit for the simple fact that I feel inadequate. I have laid my head on my pillow many nights and thought, "What am I doing? I have got to find another way; I am constantly failing our children." (And all the other moms out there said, "I feel you sister!")

I feel this way when they get a failing grade on math, when they can't spell a word they should know by now, or when our fourth grader still struggles to love reading at times.

I start to worry about where they are, where they should be, and panic about how in the world I am going to help them learn enough to go to college in the future. The homeschool mom stress is so real sometimes.

Then one day it hit me. Maybe for the same reasons our kids get antsy, frustrated, and refuse to do schoolwork are the same exact reason that I get antsy, frustrated, and scream out, "I quit!" I think sometimes our kids are worried about letting us, their parents, down just as much as we are worried about letting our kids down. Do I always think this is the case? Absolutely not! Sometimes kids are just going to be kids and simply don't want to do schoolwork. But I do believe sometimes the expectations can be so great in the home to do well in school, it can get to our kids and they act out because of the pressure we put on them.

Both of our sons have confessed to periods of frustration; frustration stemming from me fussing at them about doing something in school, confessions that they don't want to do poorly, fail, or disappoint me. They want to "make mommy happy." Ouch, right?

School is so important. Having educated children who can function well in society is huge. But when the pressure to achieve turns into this unbearable weight and starts to unravel our kid's ability to function...something needs to change.

So, what do we do when things in the home get stressful? What do we do when everyone is frustrated and hates homeschooling altogether? The biggest thing that we can do is learn the telltale signs of what it looks like when everyone is reaching the crux of, "I can't do this anymore; I quit." We have to pump the breaks and deviate before we get to that point. While I don't always catch the signs, I am doing better.

When a storm is rolling in, there are certain signs to look out for. The wind picks up, the birds are more visible to a darkened sky, the temperature drops, and thicker clouds roll in. When nature's foreshadowing begins, you know it is time to go inside and take cover. Most people aren't just going to stand outside and take the beating of the storm; they are going to do something different to protect themselves.

In the same way, we as moms have to learn what the indicators of frustration, burnout, and "I quit" look like for ourselves and our kids. We have to strive to do something about it before we all get to that point.

I know for our youngest, he gets increasingly whiny and panicked about doing his work perfectly when he is about ready to have a full-on meltdown. Our oldest starts to grip his pencils harder, erase more aggressively, and then writes with so much pressure that he breaks the head of his pencil multiple times. For me, I tend to be "on" the kids more than usual; I helicopter. When I do this, I get more frustrated with them; I catch myself pacing, cleaning the house, watching them like a hawk, and correcting every mistake I think they are making. These are all signs one—if not all of us—are about to explode.

As their mom, I have learned to read these signs and do something different before they get to the point where they want to fly off the handle and give up. There are so many things I have come up with over the years.

Lately, I do this funny thing where I go over to my children and take my hands, place them on their head and give them a "brain massage" while repeating, "brain massage, brain massage, brain massage" in a funny voice (the voice is usually different each time). They love it! Not only does it give them some time to take a quick break from school, but it also makes them laugh and helps them relax.

I will also randomly approach them, give them a kiss on the cheek, and tell them how awesome they are and how they are doing a fantastic job. Other times I will glance over their work and let them know they are crushing their lessons. If they aren't, I gently correct them, praise them for what they have gotten right so far, and encourage them to keep up the good work while giving them a big hug. It has been said you need at least ten hugs a day, ten seconds each to release all the happy hormones...so hug your family!

As for me, I have multiple tricks for when I feel like a storm is brewing inside of me. Sometimes I walk away and take some deep breaths while declaring the name of Jesus over and over again; after all, He is the ultimate peace. Other times I put my earphones in and listen to some worship music or an encouraging podcast. I have even screamed into pillows and have encouraged our kids to as well—trust me, it gives an incredible release! I will take breaks outside to breathe fresh air or take walks with the kids to give us all a nice pause. I will go into a quiet room and call a friend to check on them, so all my focus and attention isn't always on the kids.

All of these things have revolutionized our homeschool days. Do we still have bad days? Yes. Who doesn't have bad days? But I will confess learning to deviate has helped our days and our sanity tremendously.

○ ○ ○

Tips for Success #6: Leave Room for Fun

Fun is so important! Often in the homeschool life we forget this, and it is hard to just relax. We push and push because we want so much for our kids to be educated, we forget to make room for fun and laughter, but making room for these things every day is the only true way you and your family will survive the homeschool life—trust me. We cannot and should not always be so serious. We cannot let our clock-in time as "homeschool mom" cause us to forget to just be "mom" and let loose sometimes. We need to stop and laugh at our kids' jokes, make silly faces, and play with our kids.

For example, one of my favorite ways to release stress and welcome quick entertainment is to have random dance party breaks! Without warning, I will put on a song and shout, "Dance break time!" We all get up and dance like no one is watching us, and we have a blast. Furthermore, after the break everyone is so refreshed and ready to continue working with a clear, rejuvenated mind. It is so important for our children not only to work hard, but also to have fun; to see us doing these things as well. They are learning how to balance life through us and if we are always so serious and hard-pressed, they will never learn what it truly means to have a balanced life of work and fun. I don't know about you, but I don't want to be known as the mom who makes my kids feel weighed down all of the time; I want to be the mom who refreshes my kid's hearts.

Prayer:
Lord, you talk about joy a lot in your words, and so I know you desire it for your children and think that it is really important. Help me as a mom to bring joy into our homeschool days. Life and school are hard enough without me putting crazy pressure on our kids all of the time. I know you have created me as their mom to help them learn and grow, but I also know you have created me as their mom to help them let loose and show them the joy of the Lord. You are so fun, Lord! Help me to continue to reveal to our kids just how extraordinarily fun you can be.

Also, I pray that you help me notice the signs of burnout in myself and in our children so I will know when to deviate and do something different. Help me know when to pump the breaks or hit the pause button on our workload during crazy school days to make room for fun. Lord, I also plead that you would help me to invent new ways to have fun with our kids, to help relieve the pressure this world can bring.

In Jesus' Name,
Amen

Proverbs 15:13, "A joyful heart makes a face cheerful, but a sad heart produces a broken spirit."

Philemon 1:7, "For I have great joy and encouragement from your love, because the hearts of the saints have been refreshed through you, brother."

Tell Me Your Warning Signs, Momma

What are your personal warning signs that burnout is immi-
nent? What are your children's warning signs?

_____

_____

_____

_____

_____

_____

_____

_____

_____

_____

_____

_____

_____

Fill Up Your Bookshelf

Fun things to do with your children:

1. Take a dance break.
2. Take a walk/workout with them.
3. Tell jokes to each other.
4. Play hide-and-seek. Although, if you play in our house the dog always finds us first, barks, and gives away our hiding spot so the game doesn't last very long.
5. Play something they want to play.
6. Play their favorite video game.
7. Play a board game or card game for fun.
8. Play an educational board game or card game. They will have fun and they won't even realize they are learning at the same time.
9. Watch a science or educational video that goes along with what they are learning instead of reading it.
10. Turn your lesson into a discussion and figure out what your kids would do in certain situations.
11. Quiz your children and give them Nerf gun bullets for each one they get right and then have a Nerf gun war (this is a huge hit in our house).
12. Let your children run through the sprinkler.
13. Read their book aloud instead of them reading on their own.
14. Go to the Dollar Tree and let them pick out something fun to do (a puzzle, art, or let them pick out some candy for a job well done that day).
15. Surprise them with a quick trip to get their favorite treat. My boys love going to Krispy Kreme to get a donut.
16. Go to the library.
17. Go to a nearby park and let them play.

18. Ride bikes together.
19. Have a tea-time/hot chocolate break.
20. Turn snack time into "make a snack time" and let them do the making. Sometimes we make our own granola bars, cut up veggies together, or make cookies.
21. Take time to encourage one another. Take turns saying a few nice things about one another to lift each other up.
22. Let them take breaks to do what they like to do on their own... they need time away from people too.
23. Surprise them with play dates with other families...it's a fun time for all.
24. Listen to them. Give your undivided attention and let them talk about anything and everything that is on their mind. I say, "OK, you have five minutes to let it all out....and go!" Of course, I do not always put time constraints on our kids talking to me but doing it this way, the kids get a kick out of it.
25. Take hug breaks! Love your children well.

CONFESSION #7

There Are Days I Wish I Was Doing Something Else

In my life, I have had some fascinating experiences which I will forever cherish. Not only will I cherish those times, but sometimes I deeply wish I could still be a part of them. One memory my heart often longs for is working at The Lighthouse FM 89.3 in St. Marys, Georgia. That's right, your girl used to work at a Christian radio station. I started working there when I was in tenth grade. I worked for them in different capacities until I was in my early twenties. Oh, how I miss my old team; they are some of my favorite people on the planet.

During another season of my life I was a personal trainer. I loved working as a trainer. Not only do I enjoy working out, but I also found it fulfilling to help others to reach their goals. I trained people at a couple of different gyms, which made my life hectic, but it was fulfilling nonetheless. I was a personal trainer for about three years.

A couple of years ago I started to learn how to play the drums. I always wanted to be a drummer growing up, but back in the day when I was in our school band, boys were given the roles of drummers, so I had to pick a more "girly" instrument such as the clarinet. I didn't mind the clarinet, but it suppressed my inner Animal (referring to Muppets). As an adult, I thought, "You know what, you only live once on this crazy earth, I want to drum." So our youth pastor at the time taught me! I had a blast and even drummed for our youth group praise band for about a year. Sometimes when a certain song comes on, I am taken back and then I am in my own little happy place in my mind drumming away.

Although I have had some incredible opportunities, there have been many other opportunities I really do not care to return to. I have worked in retail, fast food, I was a terrible barista at one point, I worked at a golf course (which was kind of fun), and I have tried so many different at-home businesses it is almost embarrassing. I mean, what's a mom supposed to do when she is stuck at home with two kids?

Now I homeschool. So why does all of this other stuff matter?

When we have perfect homeschool days and I am caught up in all the homeschool bliss, my mind doesn't wander so much. I am completely happy and content with where I am as a homeschool mom. I encourage our kids, sing out praise and thanksgiving to God, and do everything with a smile on my face and a (somewhat) flawless attitude. Homeschooling on favorable days feels like walking outside on a cool spring day with the sunshine kissing my face and birds chirping in the background. These days nothing could convince me to do anything else.

However, in the thick of homeschool when the kids are irritable, unwilling to do schoolwork, and it feels like I am carrying them on my back up a hill covered in snow while a tiger is chasing me...these are the days my mind wanders. These are the days I wish I was doing something else, anything else; including those not-so-great opportunities I experienced!

On the difficult days I tend to let my mind daydream of all the other things I could be doing with my life instead of homeschooling. I think about all the free time I would have on my plate and everything I would accomplish if I just sent my kids back to school so someone else could take over their education. All my opened-up time could be spent writing books instead of waking up early to squeeze it in, cleaning a house that would stay clean for the most part, hanging out with friends (oh, all the girl time I could have!), or even getting a job to help our family out financially.

> ON THE DIFFICULT DAYS I TEND TO LET MY MIND DAYDREAM OF ALL THE OTHER THINGS I COULD BE DOING WITH MY LIFE INSTEAD OF HOMESCHOOLING.

I even try to figure out out-of-the-box ways to jump back into the things I loved doing, such as helping the radio station out, personal training, or wondering if the youth band at church would welcome me back in...or better yet, which at-home business I might be successful at this time? Oh, brother. All these things sound more than ideal in the middle of the miserable days.

But in my life there are two things I know God has told me to do: write and homeschool. These are the two things I have heard Him speak so clearly about. However that doesn't stop me from daydreaming and wishing I was doing something else sometimes.

Now I am not saying if you are a homeschool mom, you can't do anything else you enjoy. Having hobbies is necessary, life-giving even. I love to run and work out, do crafts, read books, listen to podcasts, and hang out with friends; I even drum sometimes for fun. Doing things you enjoy is so crucial for a homeschool mom's sanity and success.

I am also not saying if you are a homeschool mom you can't have a job doing what you love and contributing to your family's finances. I know so many moms who homeschool and own very successful home businesses. I even know homeschool moms who have full-time jobs outside of the home and homeschool their children, who are also extremely successful. Maybe you are one of those moms, and if you are, you rock! Every homeschool mom is called to her own journey; everyone also has different capacities.

For me, not only do I have to be mindful of what I say "yes" to, because I tend to say yes to way more than I can handle and eventually drown in all my responsibilities, but every time I try to do something else other than homeschooling our kids, I get this weird feeling as if something is physically holding me back.

I honestly think it is because the Holy Spirit wants to remind me He told me to homeschool. I also think He knows I tend to say yes to too many things, and when I do my children are the ones who tend to suffer—and of course my stress level increases. When I am involved in too much, it is hard for me not only to keep my head above water, but it is hard to keep my family a priority and homeschooling my kids a priority; school tends to take a back burner and our kids' education suffers.

Again, that doesn't keep me from looking back on those past projects wistfully, and it also doesn't keep new, exciting opportunities from coming or make saying no to those opportunities any easier.

Just recently an opening came up and it was so hard to say no; it was a prospect I never thought I would be given but something I had always wanted. I have always wanted to be involved in full-time ministry of some sort. When I was working at the radio station, those were the glory days.

However, God had different plans for my husband and me. The military took us away and ever since then I have been searching for my place in full-time ministry: whether that would be traveling and speaking, or working in some non-profit such as a church. Full-time ministry has always been the ultimate goal.

Last year our church was going through some organizational shifts. Our youth pastor and his family were taking the huge leap of faith to start their own church in a different city, which left a huge gap within our church. The church needed a new youth pastor. My husband and I had been active within the youth group for about four years at that point.

The pastor pulled my husband and me into his office one afternoon and gave us the news that our youth pastor was stepping down. He then proceeded to offer me the job as the youth pastor. He gave me the option of either filling in until they found someone, working part-time, or if I wanted the job full time it was mine to have. I was blown away that they wanted me and believed in me to do the job, and I was blown away my dream of being involved in ministry again was right in front of me, just waiting on a platter to be taken.

But...my kids...our kids. Working full-time or maybe even part-time would have possibly meant putting our kids back into school.

We prayed and prayed. My husband and I went back-and-forth, up-and-down through all the different scenarios on how we could make it work, working full time or even part-time and homeschooling at the same time. I prayed and prayed. I was hoping for the answer, "Yes, this is your moment, this is what you were created for, take it!" However, I never got the answer I desired.

I wanted the yes. But I got a no.

I did take the job for the summer until they found someone else to take the position. I had an unforgettable experience. However, during my time that summer, all the doubts and insecurities flooded my mind about homeschooling our kids. Will "homeschool mom" be the only thing I am ever known for? Will I ever get to do what I want to do? Will I be too old for ministry once our kids are done with school? Is God done with me? My heart and spirit were crushed.

But God.

He refocused my attention on who was right in front of me: our boys.

I was reminded that every single day I have a captive audience.

Momma, every single day, you have a captive audience.

○ ○ ○

Tips for Success #7:
Focus on Who Is Right in Front of You

Mom sitting at home, I see you. Maybe you feel like you are losing yourself in all the homeschool mess. Maybe you feel like I did: that homeschool is a place where a mom's dreams go to die. Mom, this does not have to be the case. Homeschool can be a place of personal growth, a place where God can constantly mold you into being who He created you to be—a training ground, if you will.

Over the years I have learned homeschooling is a beautiful place, where as a mom I have learned more about myself than I ever have doing anything else. Not only have I learned more about myself, I have learned more about my husband, our kids, and I have also increased in knowledge about our God.

Not to mention, God doesn't care only about the calling on your life, he cares about the calling on your husband's life, and your children's lives. You are not just a single person anymore. You are a family unit, and he wants what is best for not only you individually, but for the rest of your family both as individuals and collectively.

I thought for sure by now I would be preaching around the world, but I am not. I am in our home teaching, nurturing, preparing, and preaching to our two boys; not exactly the audience I thought I would have, but the audience that God knew needed me...the audience God knew that I needed.

While I may not grace a stage or stand behind a podium this week, I know beyond a shadow of a doubt I am where I am supposed to be. Besides, if I am supposed to be doing something else for the sake of myself, our family, and the Kingdom, God will certainly let me know.

He will let you know.

Look at who is in front of you, momma. Your family...each one of them is a gift. Be thankful for each season you have with them. They are precious gems, treasures, and they should be treated as such.

Leave behind where you thought you would be. Embrace where you are, rest in it, and be thankful.

Your audience is waiting for you.

Prayer:
Lord, I may not be where I thought I would be at this point in my life. Perhaps I thought I would be anywhere but here, but you have placed me in this home with this family for a purpose. I pray that in the hard days, the days where I am tempted to do something else, you would remind me of the gift I have in homeschooling our kids. I also pray you help me to see beyond myself. Life is not just about me anymore; it is about our entire family. Help me to serve them and love them! And I pray through everything I do for them, I pray you would help me to become all you created me to be. Help me to be thankful where I am at until you call me to do something else.

In Jesus' Name,
Amen

Psalm 127:3, "Children are a gift from the LORD;
they are a reward from him." (NLT)

Philippians 1:6, "I am sure of this, that He who started
a good work in you will carry it on to completion until
the day of Christ Jesus."

You Can Do It

What do you think are the positives to homeschooling your kids?

_____

_____

_____

_____

_____

_____

_____

_____

_____

_____

_____

_____

Fill Up Your Bookshelf

If you couldn't think of anything, here is a list just for you!

1. Your kids do not have to wake up early and ride the school bus.
2. You do not have to wake up early to get your kids ready to rush them onto the school bus.
3. You can have "God Time" with them first thing in the morning.
4. You do not have to pack lunches (unless you have community days, of course).
5. If your kids are sick, you do not have to go to the doctor to get an excuse.
6. If your kids are sick, you as the parent can let them rest and catch them up later.
7. You know what your kids are learning every single day.
8. Every moment can be a teachable moment.
9. You are your own boss! (Well, in our house my husband is the principal...lol).
10. You have control over your family's schedule (there is freedom in homeschool).
11. You can vacation whenever you want or can as a family.
12. You get to decide what is best for your children.
13. You can get the help your children need.
14. They can be involved in extracurricular activities during the day.
15. Your family can go on more field trips together.
16. Your kids are around more to do chores (the house doesn't clean itself).
17. You get to be there more often when your kids have their "aha" moments of learning.
18. You get to hug more.
19. You get to laugh more.
20. You get to love more.

CONFESSION #8

Jesus Is Not Always My Center Focus

found Jesus when I was twelve years old, almost thirteen. I had heard His name before through Sunday school and family, but this particular summer I found the real Him. The one who wanted a relationship with me and knew me by name. The one who loves me unconditionally regardless of all my past, present, or future mistakes. Because of Him, my life was forever changed.

Since that summer, I have dedicated my life to following Him and sharing Him with other people so they too could know the real Jesus. I have led Bible studies, worked in different ministries, preached, and written about His goodness so others could find Him.

So others could find Him.

When we had our boys, it was easy for me to just see them as our boys. In the beginning, I didn't see them as people who I needed to lead to Christ. To be honest I saw them as a distraction from my "real" ministry outside of the home... reaching *others* for Christ.

Did I enjoy our kids? Yes! Did I love them? Yes! But seeing them as human beings who needed my guidance to Jesus was an odd concept to me. I just figured being in a home with two Christian parents was enough. But actually leading them seemed foreign.

Not only that, but when our kids were born, we lived thirty to forty minutes from the nearest church, which meant we weren't super active in the church, and we lacked community. Also, my husband's military job at the time had him working rotating swing shifts (the worst!). At the beginning of our lives with children, we were overly tired, and barely-surviving parents of two boys. Those days were hard, lonely, and crazy (and oh, did I mention we were overly tired).

We loved Jesus but pursuing Him, serving Him, and the idea of leading our kids were all definitely on the backburner. We were just trying to keep our kids fed and alive at the time. Can I get an amen? It wasn't until the first year we attempted to homeschool our children that the lightbulb came on for me: it isn't just enough to be a Christian around our kids. We were called to lead our children to Christ.

I believe this had a lot to do with the curriculum we chose at the time. When we first started homeschooling, we were using Abeka's homeschool curriculum. In the curriculum, they included scripture cards for memorization. Our oldest was in pre-K and loved to learn his scriptures every week. He took pride in it even.

One morning while we were studying scripture the Lord tapped me on the shoulder and reminded me, *"You may not be ministering in the capacity you used to, but look at your sons in front of you; they are your ministry, they are your disciples."* This was the first time God showed me my new captive audience.

As Christians, it is so easy to get caught up in the scripture, "Go into all the world and preach the gospel to all creation," that we miss sharing the gospel to our own children (Mark 16:15, NIV).

Hey, no judgment here! I get it. For years I missed so many moments and opportunities with our kids. I could have been pouring into them spiritually, but I wasn't.

Thank God for *grace*.

The moment God tapped me on the shoulder as I was standing in front of our two sons, while one was whining and tugging on my pant leg and the other reciting a scripture he was learning, my paradigm shifted, and I became even more dedicated to the cause of Christ: *to make Him the center of our lives and to make disciples...in our own home.*

Over the course of time, I have become aware that we have two sons, disciples, who need guidance to "feel their way toward Him" (Acts 17:27, ESV). They aren't just our little boys. They are creations, image-bearers, whom God entrusted to us to grow in their knowledge of Him so that hopefully one day they will grow into men who will follow Him on their own.

I have learned the only way to make disciples of our children is

> I HAVE LEARNED THE ONLY WAY TO MAKE DISCIPLES OF OUR CHILDREN IS TO KEEP JESUS IN THE CENTER OF EVERYTHING.

to keep Jesus in the center of everything. Most would think this is especially easy in a homeschooled environment, but that is not always the case. Just like everyone else outside of the scope of homeschool, life gets busy, distractions come, and laziness is always creeping at our doorstep.

The busy life.

The beauty of homeschooling is there is so much freedom involved. However, with freedom comes an open door to so many options; as a family, we can choose to add whatever we want to our plate. But if we aren't careful, homeschool life can quickly become a crushing chaotic environment.

Just like a kid in a candy store grabbing all his favorites, it is easy to say yes to all of the communities, groups, and additional curriculum so our children can be "well-rounded kids." We can say yes to Classical Conversations, our main curriculum. We can say yes to the communities which include extracurricular activities such as chess clubs. We can say yes to all the book clubs. We can even add whatever lessons we want to our already busy schedule; piano lessons, guitar lessons, or singing/acting lessons. We can add sports into the mix as well because our kids are passionate, and we want to feed that passion. We can add *all of the things.* Our kids may get burned out, but they are learning, growing, and they are becoming well-rounded human beings, right?

However, whenever we add too much to our homeschool days, there is literally no room for Jesus (or even a deep breath). The freedom to homeschool our children is refreshing and a gift, but it can also be a double-edged sword if we aren't careful.

The distracted life.

Homeschool life is full of distractions. Not only is there danger of adding so much to our plate that our business itself becomes a distraction, but there are so many other things out there which can cause our focus to shift.

Just like any parent with kids in public school, we as homeschool parents can get easily distracted about grades, academic accomplishments, and whether or not our kids are becoming functional human beings of society. We constantly worry about their academic progress, how to keep their GPA up, and whether they'll get into college.

These questions can haunt us: Are our kids learning all they should in their education? Are they behind? Will they be behind if we continue to homeschool them? How are they compared to other kids their age?

When these doubts and fears creep in, Jesus is the last person we are thinking about. We are in the zone of making sure our kids are meeting standards we think they should be meeting at their current age, and we will do just about anything and everything to get them to "the place they should be."

The lazy life.

Attached to the busy life and the distracted life comes the lazy life. How is that even possible? Well, a lot of times we get so busy and distracted it is easy to feel overwhelmed, bogged down, and get to the point where we just want to throw our hands up in the air and quit!

I usually hit this wall way before our kids do. Our busy schedule makes me feel stressed. Our distracted life makes me feel guilty. Then I just want to scream, give up, and sleep all the time. Instead of waking up early to read the Bible and get our day going, I reach for the excuse of, "We are just so busy, I am just so tired, I need to rest; our kids need to rest. We homeschool so that if we are tired, we can sleep in and it is okay."

Rest is important, yes. However, when we are using our busy and distracted lives as an excuse to rest more than we should because we aren't making rest a priority in the first place, there is an issue.

Moreover, if we aren't making time for rest, there is a chance we are also not taking time for Jesus either.

"Let's not homeschool today, guys; let's just watch movies." Taking a rest day or a lazy day isn't a sin but oftentimes it can be easy to slip into the habit of making indolent days the norm. Then educating our kids about anything—Jesus-related or school-related—goes completely out the window.

Congratulations, instead of creating functioning humans of society who love and serve Jesus, we have created couch potatoes. Ouch!

All that being said, how do we keep Jesus in the center of our homeschool world?

The way we keep Jesus at the center of our homeschool world is to *make* Him the center of our homeschool world—which may seem like the obvious answer, but knowing and executing are two totally different things.

We can say Jesus is the center, but if we never talk about Him, never spend time with Him individually or as a family, and we never serve Him outside of the home, is He really the center?

We have to make Jesus an *unmovable* priority.

For our family, we set a schedule and put Jesus first. We wake up, have breakfast, and get into the Word and pray before we do anything else. We are not perfect at this, but it is something we are constantly striving towards each day.

We also must pay attention to how much we add to our schedule. As parents, not only are we the protectors of our children's hearts, but we are also the protectors of their schedules. If adding something to our lives doesn't leave any room for Jesus, then something's got to give, and it must be the thing that is pushing Jesus out.

Not only do we need to make Jesus a priority, but we also must ensure we are making Jesus' priorities our priorities.

Aside from making sure that our schedules aren't hectic, we have to make sure we aren't so focused on all that our kids are doing (adding all the extra things to our days) or producing (becoming distracted by grades, accomplishments, and fitting into society), that we forget to care about who are they becoming.

What good is a kid who can play piano, chess, make good grades, and become a functional human in society if they have terrible character? What good is it if we teach our kids to strive for all the other things in life but our children do not know how to love, give, or care for others? We have to teach our kids to put Jesus and His priorities in the center of all that they do. The only way to do this is to not only pursue Him as a family but pursue Him personally.

Let me explain. What good is spending time with Jesus as a family if our kids never see us pursuing Him on our own? Our kids not only need to see us making Jesus a priority for our family, but also making Him a priority for ourselves personally. They will not see the importance of making Jesus the priority of their own personal lives if they do not see us as the adult making Him a priority for our own lives.

I saw a quote once that said, "Your child will be no kinder than you are...they will not be happier than you are...and they certainly will not read the Bible if you don't." (Author Unknown)

We have to lead our kids to Jesus through our example. We must show them that not only is He vital for our family for survival, but He is vital for us personally so we can survive and thrive. He holds all things together (Colossians 1:17).

I have some questions for you, momma.

Do your kids see you reading your Bible? Do they hear you praying? Do they hear you worshipping? Do they see you actively living out what you read about in scripture? Do they see a parent who is actively portraying the heart and the character of Jesus?

Is Jesus truly the center of everything in your life?

○ ○ ○

Tips for Success #8:
Prepare for the Drift

Just like swimming in the ocean and being pulled down the beach away from our starting point, the same thing can happen in our homeschool world. We can make Jesus the center focus for everything, but then He can easily get pushed out by the busy life, the distracted life, and the lazy life. One moment we can be all about Jesus, zeroed in on Him as our main focus, and the next moment we can be so far away from Him we are like...Jesus who?

So how do we protect our families from drifting away from Jesus? Especially when the three lifestyles (busy, distracted, and lazy) can be sneaky, and they can pull us so far away from our starting point?

When you swim in the ocean, you know that drifting away from your starting point happens because of the current. So, you are prepared to protect yourself from the drift. You pay attention to where you are at all times and make sure you aren't far from where you started. You learn to dig your heels into the sand, so you don't move far from your starting point. You surround yourself with people to make sure they too are looking out for where you are the entire time. You are alert and pay attention to warning signs you are drifting away.

In homeschool life, we can employ the exact same principles and techniques. Drifting away will most likely happen, so you prepare for it.

1. You keep your eyes on Jesus (your starting point).
2. You set boundaries (dig your heels into the sand) for the amount of how much your family can handle as far as adding things to the schedule, and at point 'X', is when you are going to say no to adding anything else to your schedule.
3. You have people (watching you) who hold you accountable for where you are and what you are doing. For example, my husband might express, "So, it's been like three days, are you guys going to do any schoolwork today?
4. You are on the constant lookout for warning signs that you are drifting.

When it comes to my family our major warning sign tends to be our speech. When I hear our kids confess, "I am stressed out, I can't do this, I just want to sleep, I can't focus," then we are probably doing too much. If our kids start hearing me declare (yes, they hold me accountable), "I just can't handle you guys, we need to rethink this homeschool thing, I don't know if I can do this anymore," then we are probably doing too much. Or if our speech is negative consistently, then something isn't right. Yes, everyone has bad days but if we are being negative for days on end, then it is time to reevaluate our lives.

Keeping Jesus front in center is vital for surviving and thriving in everyday life and especially in homeschool life. With everything that is in you, momma, fight; do all that you can to protect and keep your family from drifting away from what truly matters.

Prayer:

Lord, as a family we want to keep you at the center of everything. We pray you would help us to keep our eyes on you. We pray you help us to develop boundary lines and stick to them no matter what we want to do. We pray you will bring people into our lives who will hold us accountable to our goal to keep Jesus the center. We also pray you help us stay alert and on the lookout for warning signs if we start drifting. And, God, if we do drift, we pray that you forgive us and give us the wisdom to know what we need to let go of to get back on track and the strength to do it! We love you, Lord, and we always will.

In Jesus' Name,
Amen

> Deuteronomy 6:5-7, "Love the Lord your God with all your heart, with all your soul, and with all your strength. These words that I am giving you today are to be in your heart. Repeat them to your children. Talk about them when you sit in your house and when you walk along the road, when you lie down and when you get up."

> Hebrews 12:1-2, "Therefore, since we also have such a large cloud of witnesses surrounding us, let us lay aside every weight and the sin that so easily ensnares us. Let us run with endurance the race that lies before us, keeping our eyes on Jesus, the source and perfecter of our faith, who for the joy that lay before Him endured a cross and despised the shame and has sat down at the right hand of God's throne."

Colossians 1:17, "He is before all things, and by Him all things hold together."

Revelations 2:4, "But I have this against you: You have abandoned the love you had at first."

Make a Plan

What are the warning signs of drifting in your home? Make a plan for how you are going to keep Jesus in the center. Jot down some names of people who could help hold you accountable.

_____

_____

_____

_____

_____

_____

_____

_____

_____

_____

_____

_____

Fill Up Your Bookshelf

List of ideas and books to help keep you and your family focused.

1. We love the Bible Project (bibleproject.com).
2. As a family, read one chapter of the New Testament and a chapter of the Old Testament every day.
3. Read a Psalm or a Proverb a day as a family.
4. Memorize Scripture together.
5. Quiz each other on learned scripture.
6. Write scripture verses in a special journal.
7. Have a coloring journal where you write scripture on one side and then draw a picture on the other side interpreting the scripture.
8. Act out scriptures or Bible stories.
9. Retell stories of the Bible with funny voices.
10. Use scripture during disciplining your children. Remind your kids, what does the Word say?
11. Encourage your children with scripture.
12. Build Minecraft worlds based on scripture (our kids LOVE this!).
13. Have your kids write encouraging letters to friends and family and have them include scripture.
14. Have scripture written and placed in different areas around the house.
15. Play worship music a lot.
16. Play praise music and dance together (got to love those dance breaks).
17. Read Bible-based books together. The books below are ones we have personally read as a family and enjoyed:
    1. *The Power of Your Words* by Tony Evans
    2. *The Armor of God* by Tony Evans
    3. *The Names of God* by Tony Evans
    4. *The Battlefield of the Mind for Kids* by Joyce Meyer
18. Pray together about everything.

CONFESSION #9

I Don't Like to Ask for Help

I don't sit well. I never have. Productivity has always been extremely important to me and over the years a long list of to-dos has been one of my closest companions. I am not sure where this idea came from but all I know is when I am lounging around on the couch in my comfy clothes doing nothing, I get very uncomfortable. When my head hits the pillow at night, I like to know I gave the day my all and I accomplished something; that no time was wasted. We only get one life on this earth, right?

The problem with my love for accomplishing things is oftentimes I find myself trapped in the same cycle. I make a long list of to-dos. I mark tasks off the list. I feel fulfilled for a moment, but instead of just marking projects off and feeling good about it, I add more things to the list. Over time I create this long list for myself which I will never be able to complete.

Sometimes I have even tried to get multiple things done at once: cook dinner, while I make lunches for the next day, fold pieces of laundry in between, while simultaneously teaching one of our sons how to do his math lesson—all the while failing miserably at it, and eventually burning dinner in the process. Then instead of feeling accomplished when I go to bed at night, I spend the night lying awake thinking about how much of a failure I am because I couldn't keep up with everything. I stress over burning dinner yet again, and how I shouldn't have gotten upset at our son for not understanding his math lesson when *I* didn't even understand his math lesson.

I have learned this way of living is tremendously toxic. I have learned in life there will always be a list of things that need to be done: every day, week, month, and year. There will always be laundry and dishes, dinners to cook, and school lessons to complete. Always. The problem isn't that there are tasks that need completing or that I enjoy marking things off of my list; after all, who doesn't like the feeling of completing something? The problems come when I constrict myself to impossible time limits on finishing projects, I try to get too many things done at once, or when I am exceedingly prideful in asking for help.

My mom has told me numerous times, "Tiffany, you don't have an 'S' on your chest, you know. The way you are living will eventually catch up to you. Trust me, I know from experience."

She has been right time and time again. I have experienced burnout, sickness, and frustration; all of which did not make me a better person, but bitter, broken and stressed. In my attempt to seem stronger to myself and others, I have just ended up face-down on the ground, shattered, trying to pick up the pieces.

When I have become shattered in the past, it has not only affected me personally, but it has imposed hardship on those closest to me, my family. They get the brunt of it all. They get the tired, ill-tempered, overstretched me who can't function or give my best self to things they actually may need help with. They suffer when I suffer.

I have learned I can't do it all alone and this knowledge has led me to accept three main truths: it is not a big deal if everything isn't always done, asking for help is important, and I cannot micromanage people when I do ask for help.

I have learned everything doesn't always have to be done all the time.

There used to be a day when leaving a job unfinished was like this dark cloud that followed me around. I couldn't find joy unless I thought everything was thoroughly done for the day. I had to get up at a certain time, read my Bible, work out, take care of all things related to the house, take care of kids, walk the dogs (they need exercise too), cook a healthy meal, and even prepare things for the next day.

When something was left undone or the day didn't unfold the way I expected it to, I became unraveled. I would walk around the house angry and unsettled. The laundry that was still not put away would taunt me, the dishes in the sink would make my skin crawl, and if our babies were unbathed for the evening it was grueling going to bed at night.

Over time I have calmed down a lot, but it did not happen with ease. Through the years, all the frustrations, the letdowns, and gentle constant reminders from my husband to "just relax," won out, and little by little, I started to realize as a young mom that no matter how much I strived for perfection,

I would never obtain it. Life is messy living in a house with a family; life is full of the unexpected.

There are nights when a child wakes up sick in the middle of the night, so it's hard to wake up early the next morning to spend time with Jesus. There are days when my body gives out and I hurt myself working out, and then I can't work out for weeks. There will be days where the washing machine will break, and the laundry can't be finished for the day or even days. There will be days that are jam-packed with so much to do, the dishes in the sink will have to wait until the next day.

I have learned to accept some days all the laundry will be done but the rest of the house will suffer. There are days when I get up early to spend time with Jesus and other days when I am up at night with a sick child instead, praying over them and spending time with Jesus until they fall asleep. I have learned to accept that my body isn't as young as it used to be and sometimes, I will hurt it somehow working out and I will have to give it the rest it needs. Sometimes all our school-work gets done and other days when we just get math done because that was the main subject of struggle for that day.

Life is unpredictable, chaotic, but life is beautiful, and it is okay if things are left *undone* sometimes.

Undone. It's so uncomfortable when things are left undone, but I have noticed when I try to live my life in complete per-fection it puts so much stress and pressure on our family, especially our kids. They see me, their mom, stressing to get everything done, and then they feel like if they leave things undone, they too have somehow failed.

I realized this truth just recently, as a matter of fact. My oldest son and I were looking over his list of things he had completed for school for the day. We scanned the list together.

"Bud, what have you been doing today? You still have math, geography, and analogies to do. You still have so much to do to finish your day."

My son's words surprised me. In his infinite twelve-year-old wisdom he responded, "Mom, can we not look at all I still have to finish? Look at all I have completed. Let's look at the positives here. I don't always want to focus on what I have left to do."

Ouch! He was so right.

When we're focused on all we have left to do, it is hard to live in celebration of the things we have accomplished. Not only that but it is a stressful way to live when we constantly exist in a state of "I still have **WE MUST LEARN TO LIVE IN A STATE OF REST, THANKSGIVING, AND BEING ENOUGH; INSTEAD OF A STATE OF RUSH, PANIC, AND CONSTANT LACK.** *all* this to do." We must learn to live in a state of rest, thanksgiving, and being enough; instead of a state of rush, panic, and constant lack.

I have learned that it is imperative I ask for help.

"I need help."

Those words do not come out of my mouth easily. I like to know I can accomplish anything and everything on my own.

Not only is this way of living destructive but it is also very lonely, frustrating, and unbalanced.

Lonely. Frustrating. Unbalanced.

When I am tending to my long list of to-dos and I don't ask for help, I feel lonely. I throw myself an internal pity party while everyone else gets to be together, relax, but poor-old-mom is by herself cleaning and doing everything that "needs to get done."

My emotions don't just stop at loneliness; they quickly turn to frustration and anger. I get angry when I am the only one in the house who is still on her feet attending to and getting things done. When I am still working and everyone else is kicking back and relaxing it makes me want to explode.

My frustration morphs into an unbalanced life. When I am attending to my long list and not handing out any responsibilities to anyone else, burnout quickly follows. When I try to handle everything on my own, I don't leave any room for rest. I just keep going, running on fumes until I crash and burn.

But no one else in the house has any idea I am experiencing burnout, because I don't reveal anything at all; when, truth be told, if I asked for help my family would be more than willing because they want to help me.

Ultimately, I have grasped that asking for help is not only vital for my sanity, health, and the overall function of our home, but it is essential for the growth and development of our kids.

Our children need to know our house doesn't function on the work of the mother alone. They need to learn running a household is a team effort. The house shouldn't succeed because of a mom who thinks she is a "supermom" with a giant "S" on her chest, but on a "super family" who works remarkably as a team.

Additionally, the more I ask for help, the more sensitive our children become to seeing my signs of struggle. Lately, our oldest has been hands-down exceptional at asking, "Mom, is there anything I can help you with right now?" My husband and I are still working on our youngest with this, but he is coming along. Both our children are becoming sensitive to the needs of others and that is paramount.

They have also grown in the knowledge that it is quite all right to ask for help. They don't have to be perfect. They don't have to sit and struggle and pretend like everything is okay. They don't have to feel less-than when they reach out for help. They can live life in full confidence knowing they are not alone. They don't have to grow up feeling lonely, frustrated, and experience burnout. They are growing up knowing what it looks like to have a balanced, toxic-free life, living with a family that helps each other out daily, which is an important lesson to learn because hopefully in the future they will have a family of their own.

I have learned it is crucial to not micromanage those who give me help.

I had a hard time adjusting to the fact that not everything had to be done, and an even harder time asking for help, but the *greatest* thing I struggled with was letting go of micromanaging those who do give me help.

Just recently my husband was cooking dinner. I was tired and exhausted, and I was so thankful he was cooking dinner. However, instead of sitting down and relaxing, I was in the kitchen telling him, a thirty-eight-year-old man, how to cook hamburgers.

"Be careful not to get hamburger juice on the counter. Make sure the burgers are cooked all the way through. Please be sure to clean up after you are done."

He gave me one of his *looks* and it quickly enlightened me on what I was doing to him.

"Oh, babe I am so sorry...thank you for cooking! I am going to go sit down now."

The purpose of asking for help isn't to continue to stress. The purpose of asking for help is so others can help carry the weight of life. When I ask for help but then continue to "help" I am not only creating more work for myself, but I am also annoying the person who chooses to help me.

Besides, if I ask someone to do something for me and then I constantly harp on how they are doing it incorrectly, or I go behind them and "do it better," eventually they are going to throw their hands up and decide not to help me at all. Eventually, they will feel inadequate, or worse, may even believe that I'm disappointed by the help they're so generously giving me.

I have had to face this truth time and time again in my marriage. My husband and I have had many conversations about the fact my husband feels that even when he does help, it isn't good enough for me. Talk about a hard truth to accept. I haven't mastered the art of backing off overnight, but it has been such a necessary lesson to learn for the sake of my entire family; yes, even with our kids.

There is a fine line between teaching our kids how to do certain projects around the house to help the family, and micromanaging how they do those projects. As a mom, it is my job to teach them how to vacuum, clean their room properly, do laundry, and so much more. But I have to be mindful of how I respond when they do help but don't necessarily complete tasks in adherence to my crazy OCD standards.

One afternoon after we finished school, I asked our youngest to vacuum downstairs. He was so happy to help. He joyfully grabbed the vacuum, plugged it in, and went to town. He finished and then went back upstairs to finish cleaning his room. After he went back upstairs, I looked around and noticed he missed a few spots. I started the vacuum back up and proceeded to go over the so-called "missed spots."

I heard his footsteps pounding on the floor over the roar of the vacuum, "Mom, why are you vacuuming? I just finished doing that." I turned the machine off, walked over, and looked at his defeated face. I felt horrible.

"I am sorry buddy, but there were some spots you missed." He buried his chin to his chest and walked back to his room.

There is a difference between teaching my son how to vacuum, or showing him how he can improve at an important household chore, versus me redoubling his efforts right after he completes a job and making him feel inadequate. He is ten years old. There is no way he is going to do it exactly to my standards. But teaching him, letting him accomplish a goal, and making him feel accomplished in reaching that goal are all extremely important.

The truth is there will always be some dirt left of the floor. There will always be a piece of dirty laundry. There will always be a dish somewhere in the house that needs to be cleaned. There will always be some incomplete lessons in school. Even though all these things are true, it doesn't mean that a house has to be full of panic and chaos.

A home can be full of love, joy, and peace if every member learns to-do lists don't always have to be fully completed, it is essential to ask for help, and not to micromanage one another when help is offered.

○ ○ ○

Tips for Success #9:
Welcome the Help

Homeschool life is extremely chaotic and challenging every single day. Aside from trying to get schoolwork done, there is a house to clean, laundry to do, dinners to cook, doctor's appointments to go to, extracurricular activities to attend to, and a house to clean again once everyone has destroyed it for the entire day of doing all said schoolwork, housework, and playtime. If I am being honest, there are days I just want to pull my hair out because it is so hard to get everything done, which is why it has been so momentous for me to learn the importance of "togetherness."

Alone I can get through very little without feeling over-whelmed and defeated. But together, as a family, we can get through just about anything that comes our way.

If our house is destroyed and it needs to be cleaned, we can blast some tunes through the speakers, roll up our sleeves and have the house cleaned in a couple of hours. If we are struggling with school and dinner preparations are lacking, I can ask my husband to start cooking while I finish up with the kiddos. If we have multiple errands to run, such as doc-tor's appointments, and the house is neglected for the day, together we can admit, "Well, we did our best today, better luck tomorrow." There is power in togetherness.

Am I saying that we are exemplary at the concept? Absolutely not! There are days we struggle, fight, get on each other's nerves, and days that everything still doesn't get done. However, the beauty in the togetherness is we win together, fail together, and keep pushing forward even after we fall short...together.

Maybe you are reading this and think, "Good for you, Tiffany, you have a family to lean on. My case isn't quite like yours."

Maybe your situation isn't like mine. Maybe you are a single mom, or your husband works crazy hours and most every-thing falls on you. First, you are a superstar! Second, if you do not have much of a family or spouse you can lean on inside of the home, I want to encourage you to still welcome help.

Help comes in all different ways. Help doesn't have to come just from inside of the home.

I was enlightened to this truth last summer when my husband got Covid-19. Well, we all got it, but it hit him the worst out of all of us. Our entire house pretty much shut down. We didn't get much schoolwork done, although we tried. Most of our days were just spent making sure everyone took their vitamins, was eating healthy, and trying to keep my husband healthy and help our children and me to stay healthy. I was exhausted! Our pastor's wife reached out and asked if there is anything they could do to help.

I hesitated.

I didn't want to ask for help. I wanted to pretend like I had everything under control. However, I was desperate.

"Yes, can you please reach out to the hospitality team and set up a meal train? I feel like I am drowning here."

Friends, let me tell you that was one of the absolute greatest decisions I had ever made! When the food started to come, a huge weight lifted off my shoulders. We were fed, taken care of, and I was able to focus on our family.

Mom, regardless of your situation, I guarantee there are people in your life right now who would love to help you. All you have to do is gain the courage to ask; asking isn't always easy and it is definitely a humbling experience, but it is so important.

Even if it is just simply having one of your children fold a load of laundry a day, just ask and allow them to do it. Your laundry may not be perfectly folded but hey, it will be folded!

Maybe one of your kids is having trouble with math and you are the only teacher in your home. There has to be someone in your life circle who knows how to do math like a boss, and could help your child.

You are a fantastic mom; however, you are not a superhuman.

You need help. Welcome the help!

Prayer:
Lord, I know I need help and I cannot do everything on my own. Even though I know this for a fact, it is not always easy for me to ask for or accept help. I often believe I don't need anyone else; I believe I have an "S" on my chest and can handle it all. However, when I put on my so-called superhero cape, frustration and burnout quickly follow. Lord, please open my eyes to those around me who are ready to offer assistance and give me strength to lay down my pride and allow others to step into my life and lend a helping hand. Help me to be humble, help me to be wise, and help me to welcome the help.

In Jesus' name,
Amen

> Exodus 18:14, "When Moses' father-in-law saw all that Moses was doing for the people, he asked, 'What are you really accomplishing here? Why are

you trying to do all this alone while everyone stands around you from morning till evening?'" (NLT)

Proverbs 11:2, "When pride comes, disgrace follows, but with humility comes wisdom."

Romans 12:5, "in the same way we who are many are one body in Christ and individually members of one another."

"Be strong enough to stand alone, smart enough to know when you need help, and brave enough to ask for it."

~Ziad K. Abdelnour

"Refusing to ask for help when you need it is refusing someone the chance to be helpful."

~Ric Ocasek

Consider This

Do you know where you struggle and need the most help? If you don't know where you need help, make a list of all of your duties. Scale them to how you think you are doing (1-5; 1 meaning you need help, sister). In the places you are lacking...ask for help in those areas.

_____

_____

_____

_____

_____

_____

_____

_____

_____

_____

_____

Fill Up Your Bookshelf

Ways to schedule help and to organize your chaos:

1. Write out a chore chart for your children. There are age-appropriate lists of chores that you can easily find online.
2. Write out a list of things your husband can help you with (daily/weekly). If you are not married, figure out who in your circle can help you where you need it the most every week.
3. Write out a cleaning schedule for yourself as far as the things you will clean on certain days, so you do not feel bogged down in cleaning the entire house every single day.
4. Set up a daily schedule for yourself for everything else in your life.
5. During the summer, plan out the school year for your children as much as possible. I promise it will make your homeschool days go so much smoother.
6. Once a week, make a daily school plan for your children that they can physically hold and check off themselves. When you make a plan, it takes out the guesswork of all your kids need to accomplish. Plus, it takes away from the "Mom, what do I do next?" It doesn't take it away completely but if my kids do ask, I just say, "Look at your daily schedule."
7. If there is enough variance in your children's ages, set up a subject where the oldest can help the younger siblings. Not only does this give your oldest a sense of accomplishment, but you are also teaching your youngest to receive help from other people who aren't you. You will also free up some of your time.

8. If you have children in multiple grades, choose subjects that you can teach them all together. For example, say you choose to teach them science together. You can go over the lesson and then give your children different things to do depending on their skill level. If you taught about the solar system; a kindergartener could draw the solar system, a third grader could write a paragraph and draw the solar system as well, a middle school or high school student could do a research paper about the solar system.

9. Write out a meal plan—which is not my favorite thing to do at all—but it really makes my days a lot easier. Even if I move meals around on my two-week list of meal ideas, at least I have some kind of plan in place, so I am not having to think about what we are going to eat every single day.

10. Grocery pick-up. I told myself I would never do this, but I am so glad I started doing it! There are so many grocery stores that offer this service, and it is a huge blessing.

11. Just breathe. Life isn't perfect and it never will be.

*Please do not try to put all of these in place at once, you will stress yourself out! Pick one, master that, and then move on to incorporate something else. It hast taken us years to work all of these into our schedule and we still haven't mastered all of them.

CONFESSION #10

I Don't Always See Breakthrough

Exhausted, with tired, damaged feet, the Israelites stood with unsettled spirits as the walls of Jericho towered in front of them. The impenetrable walls and the people within the walls were what was keeping them from the Promised Land, which God declared would be theirs. They were unsure how they were going to overtake the city before them, but then God spoke to Joshua and told them exactly what to do. He gave him specific instructions:

> The LORD said to Joshua, "Look, I have handed Jericho, its king, and its fighting men over to you. March around the city with all the men of war, circling the city one time. Do this for six days. Have seven priests carry seven ram's-horn trumpets in front of the ark. But on the seventh day, march around the city seven times, while the priests blow the trumpets. When there is a prolonged blast of the horn and you hear its sound, have all the people give a mighty shout. Then the city wall will collapse, and the people will advance, each man straight ahead.
> Joshua 6:2-5

Obviously, I do not know exactly what was going through the minds of those who were commanded to march, but if I had to guess I would think they were infuriated. They had been in the desert for forty years, walking, slamming their feet to the ground because of the sins of the generation before them. They were tired and hoping after crossing the waters of the Jordan River they would finally be able to take a break. The Lord promised he would drive out their enemies before them, but to have to walk even more in order to make that happen?

I am sure marching was the last thing they wanted to do after the years of walking they put in, but that is what the Lord commanded them to do in order to take over the city of Jericho. They obeyed, kept going, and on the seventh day, the seventh time around, the final step was taken along with a prolonged blast of trumpets, and followed by their mighty shouts. The ground rumbled beneath their feet and the city walls crumbled before them.

Breakthrough.

After forty years of walking and seven days of marching around a city, a breakthrough finally transpired. But that isn't where their story ended. Even after their advancement in the city of Jericho, they had to continue to fight for the land they were promised to receive from the Lord.

Continue to fight for what was theirs.

A lot of times in our lives we want breakthrough, we want

> A LOT OF TIMES IN OUR LIVES WE WANT BREAKTHROUGH, WE WANT VICTORY, BUT WE DO NOT WANT TO PUT IN THE WORK IN ORDER TO SEE THE BREAKTHROUGH HAPPEN.

victory, but we do not want to put in the work in order to see the breakthrough happen. Not to mention the additional work which may be needed in order to see change accomplished. We want everything to materialize instantly and with little effort.

I have noticed this in my boys in the subjects where they struggle the most in school. For my oldest son, Aaron really struggles in math. Since he has dysgraphia and dyslexia this comes as no surprise. However, just because he struggles with math does not mean he doesn't need to understand it, but pushing through until he masters something can be difficult.

There have been many days the sentiment from our oldest has been, "Do we really have to go over this concept again? If I didn't understand it the last ten times, what makes you think I will understand it this time?"

Sometimes no words have to be spoken. Sometimes he grips his pencil tighter, writes with more force on the paper, and punctures holes in his work. Other times he puts out a huff and a puff as if he is going to "blow the house down." I know when he is done.

He gets frustrated. I get frustrated. Both of us have wanted to give up and just wash our hands of math forever.

Despite our frustration with math, we keep chipping away at it. We may take a break, step back, take a different approach sometimes but no matter what we keep trying. Why? Because of the beautiful day when we take that one last step, the walls crumble, a breakthrough happens, and he finally understands.

When he finally understands a concept, the look of accomplishment on his face, the sigh of relief in his breath, and the pride he feels within is priceless. We realize in the moments of breakthrough that all the work, all the pain (yes, sitting with a seventh grader doing math can be painful sometimes), and all the tears were worth it.

Usain Bolt, known as the fastest man alive, once challenged, "I trained 4 years to run only 9 seconds. There are people who do not see results in 2 months, give up and leave. Sometimes failure is sought by oneself."

Ouch!

His words could not be more true, especially in the culture we live in today. We live in a culture that wants it now and if there is any opposition, we retreat, give up, and find something else to do which may come easier to us. We want to find things that come naturally to us, so we do not have to put much effort into the things that do not.

Now, that being said, do I believe our kids will be perfect geniuses at everything? No! I am fully aware both of our sons have strengths and weaknesses, but I do not want them to use their weaknesses as an excuse to give up.

I am sure when the Israelites crossed over the Jordan River with their weakened bodies and faced the walls of Jericho, their brains immediately thought, "Nope, not today, Satan." But to take what God had set apart for them, it was imperative they kept fighting against the desire to walk away and push forward instead while relying on God's strength.

The truth is our oldest needs to understand math, whether or not it is his favorite. He may not understand every single concept in the subject, but for him to make it in life, math is vital.

So we keep working to figure out ways for him to understand it with more ease so he can be successful. Now, for our youngest, math isn't a struggle for him; reading is where he struggled for the longest time, and obviously reading is extremely important.

Straight up, I thought he would never read. I am not sure why reading was such a challenge for him, but it was so hard to sit and listen to him struggle. I may sound like a terrible person, but it truly was. I have always confessed that it seemed our oldest came out of the womb reading, so to have a struggling reader in the house was difficult.

For years (kindergarten, first, second, and some of third) he pitched many fits over sitting and reading with me. Part of the reason was that the kid hates sitting still. Getting him to sit still long enough to read was like trying to cage a cheetah. When I would finally get him to sit still, every single word took so long for him to understand and read. The weird thing was, he was gifted at phonics but for some reason, having a book in hand threw all of that out the window.

Finally, a day came when I just gave up. He wouldn't stop freaking out about reading and so I declared, "Okay, you don't want to read? I understand! When you decide that you want to learn to read let me know. But until then I am not going to force you to do it anymore." Yep, I confess, there was a time I quit helping my son learn how to read. I never thought trying to help teach a kid to read would break me, but it did.

After taking a step back from forcing him to read, I started to think about his interests. He loves alligators. I did some digging and I found a series of kid books called "Investigators" and purchased them for him. The books became one of his Christmas presents. I was optimistically hopeful he would want to read them. There had been many other books and series I bought hoping to spark his interest, which I tried to read with him or get him to read on his own, and they just sat on the bookshelf and collected dust.

But Christmas came, he opened his books, and he could not wait to read them. I was shocked! He sat with them and took off with his "newly found, newly discovered" love for reading books.

Breakthrough.

The moments when breakthroughs happen, when the light-bulb finally comes on for our kids after they have struggled with something for so long, is one of the most considerable joys of homeschooling them.

However, in the middle, when my husband and I are in the trenches fighting with them for some kind of progress, it can be maddening. There have been so many instances when my husband and I have been helping our boys and all we wanted to do is bang our heads against the wall.

The main reason isn't that we do not want to help our children comprehend and succeed, but more so because we want them to comprehend and succeed on our timeline. We want the breakthroughs to happen when we want them to.

As a matter of fact, we are all like this with almost every aspect of our lives. We see a goal, we make a timeline for ourselves, and when we do not reach the created deadline when we think we should, we fall apart and retreat.

What if the Israelites quit marching around the walls of Jericho on the seventh day, the seventh time around, right before the last step? The answer is a given. The walls would have never crumbled, and the Israelites would have never gotten to the Promised Land.

A lot of times, we put a stop to reaching our goals because we stop pursuing them. Just as Usain Bolt warned, "Sometimes failure is sought by oneself." We give up too soon. We give up right before the breakthrough materializes.

Over time I have learned our children are not always going to do things or learn things on my preconceived timelines. They may get something as early as today or it may be ten years from now before they fully understand. That doesn't mean I stop putting in the work. I just have to continue to put in the work until they do understand.

We have to submit our timelines to God, and we have to keep fighting alongside our children no matter how long it takes. We have to trust the process, and realize that even when our breakthrough feels forty years away, it's still coming. And we *must* keep marching.

○ ○ ○

Tips for Success #10:
Keep Marching

Are you currently marching around the walls of a struggle your child is having? Do you feel like you have been circling around the same situation for way too long and you just want to retreat? I want to encourage you today: do not give up. Keep marching, my friend.

Why?

Your children need you to fight for them and beside them. They need you to believe in them no matter the circumstances. They need you to be a cheerleader walking beside them, chanting encouraging words in their ears, and helping them to believe in themselves so they can become successful.

They will encounter enough negativity in their lives, and they need you to be the voice of positivity. They will have enough people in their lives shouting them down, belittling them, telling them to give up and that they "will never understand, get better, or have a breakthrough." They will have enough people walking away and giving up on them. Do not let that be you!

Trust me, it is so easy to want to throw in the towel. I have been there. However, your kids need you to be the person who has the strength to carry on when they want to give up themselves.

Even if it seems like they are behind in a certain area and we feel as if we are carrying them on our worn-out shoulders, that doesn't give us as parents' permission to weasel out and give up on our children or to pressure them in a scathing manner. Yes, society has come up with a system to dictate where your child should be by a certain age and grade. Systems aren't terrible and they are there for a reason. However, we cannot let those systems push us to put unnecessary stress on our children to adhere to that timeline.

Homeschool isn't a place where we put our children in a box and force our timelines as parents or societies timelines on them, inevitably causing them to feel brainless or inadequate. On the contrary, homeschool should be a safe place to give our children the freedom, the space, and the confidence for them to learn they are capable—even if it takes them years to understand a concept. Homeschool should be a place where we teach them if they keep working at their areas of struggle, eventually, breakthroughs will happen.

Prayer:
Lord, there are so many days and moments in this homeschool journey I want to quit, especially when it feels like we have walked around the same walls for so long. I pray no matter how hard it gets, no matter how many times I want to retreat, I pray you give me the energy and the strength to walk alongside our children and to keep fighting on their behalf. Help me to see their areas of struggle as an opportunity for you to work in our lives instead of a burden. Also, help me to not rely solely on the timelines I have placed on them, or society has placed on them. Please Lord, help me to trust your timeline for them and to keep striving until a breakthrough happens.

In Jesus' Name,
Amen

Joshua 6:20, "So the people shouted, and the trumpets sounded. When they heard the blast of the trumpet, the people gave a great shout, and the wall collapsed. The people advanced into the city, each man straight ahead, and they captured the city."

2 Chronicles 15:7, "But as for you, be strong; don't be discouraged, for your work has a reward."

Isaiah 40:29-31, "He gives strength to the weary and strengthens the powerless. Youths may faint and grow weary, and young men stumble and fall, but those who trust in the LORD will renew their strength; they will soar on wings like eagles; they will run and not grow weary; they will walk and not faint.

1 Corinthians 9:24, "Don't you know that the runners in a stadium all race, but only one receives the prize? Run in such a way to win the prize.

Be Honest

What are some areas your children are currently struggling in? Have you wanted to stop helping them in these areas? What can you do to keep advancing forward?

_____

_____

_____

_____

_____

_____

_____

_____

_____

_____

_____

_____

_____

Fill Up Your Bookshelf

Here are some steps to take if your child is struggling in an area:

1. Press Pause: In the middle of a struggle when frustration is high, it is so easy to lash out and respond with something negative instead of expressing uplifting words to your child. Take a step back and take a deep breath before you respond. Sometimes it is even necessary to walk away and then come back when you have calmed down and are ready to respond with more encouragement.

2. Give some space: Take some time away from the struggle. You have to give yourself permission to take a break from the struggle; taking a break does not mean you are giving up. I have had to do this multiple times. I have taken a week, two weeks, or even a month of a break from a concept my children may be struggling with and then revisit it with fresh eyes. Not to mention the fact that sometimes kids just need a brain break from their areas of struggle; their brains just need time to process the concept.

3. Take another approach: There have been many times I have helped our oldest son with a math concept over and over again and he still did not get it. But I realized it was because each time we would go over it, I would explain it the same way. If your child is not getting a concept, think of another way you can present the information so maybe they will understand it better; maybe even make it into a game or a conversation instead of taking the same old approach.

4. Encourage your child and then encourage them some more: The world is not short of negativity. Our children will receive all kinds of hate from so many people in their lives. The last place they need to hear negative talk or constant belittlement, is from their parents.

5. Relax: If it's at all possible, relax. Eventually, your child will understand what you are trying to help them with. No, it may not be on your timeline, but it will eventually happen.

CONFESSION #11

Despite It All, Homeschooling Is My Favorite

When I was ten years old, the oldest of my brothers (I have three) took me to Six Flags Over Georgia for the first time. I was terrified to ride roller coasters because I had never ridden one before. Absolutely terrified! But being a brother, he didn't care if I was frightened or not. He loved roller coasters and wanted me to love them too!

The first ride he took me on was the Georgia Cyclone. The roller coaster was this old wooden roller coaster that had an alarming drop of one hundred feet in the air. I reluctantly got in line with him and his wife and waited while my body shook in fear.

Our time came. We stepped onto the ride, got strapped in, I cried a ridiculous amount, and the ride began. Did the crying stop? Nope! I cried and cried the entire ride, and I couldn't wait to get off that death trap. Needless to say, I didn't ride another roller coaster the rest of the day or for an extremely long time.

A long time! Twenty-five years to be exact.

Just recently my husband and I were able to get away for some much-needed alone time. Our summer had not been fun at all. We spent the summer getting over the dreaded Covid (if you know, you know), our dog had knee surgery, our oldest had oral surgery, my husband worked a lot, I spent tons of time getting homeschool stuff ready for the year, and we were just spent. Thankfully all was well on one particular weekend and my in-laws came over so we could have some much-needed time together: thanks Meme and Pops!

The entire weekend my most gracious husband did everything I wanted to do. We went shopping (even though he knew I didn't need *anything* else in my closet), enjoyed yummy Starbucks multiple times, went to Billy Graham's Library, and ate at fantastic restaurants. He just kept asking me what I wanted to do.

Except for this one time we were trying to figure out what to do and he uttered the words, "Let's go ride some roller coasters."

He knew how much I hated them. He followed up with, "Nah, I'm just kidding, I know you do not want to do that!" Of course, I didn't want to ride roller coasters, but I didn't want to make the trip all about me.

Unenthusiastically, under my breath, I responded, "We can go ride roller coasters."

"Really?!" Fantastic, I got his hopes up.

"Yes, we can go, I don't want to make the trip all about me."

"Babe, I know you hate them, it is okay! We don't have to go ride them." Shew, I dodged that bullet...or so I thought.

We woke up the next day and he suggested, "After church let's go to Carowinds! It is something different, we will have fun."

My insides did flips. I whined about it, a considerable amount. But I already agreed I would go so I knew nothing I said would change his mind and we were going to go.

"I promise I won't make you do anything you don't want to do. But just try one."

Just one? Just one! He might as well have been asking me to jump out of an airplane. But I was committed. I seriously did want to do something he enjoyed. We got to the park, and it wasn't too crowded. Although it wasn't crowded, I saw the invisible walls drawing in closer and I felt claustrophobic.

The roller coasters were *huge*. I wanted to vomit.

"This one isn't that big. Let's do this one!" my husband encouraged me.

The roller coaster was called Vortex. On this particular roller coaster, you had to stand up as you ride. There were multiple twists and turns, but it did seem like the shortest ride timewise and the "smallest" mid-sized roller coaster.

We stood in line. I panicked more and more the closer we got to the front of the line; playing all of the horrible scenarios out in my mind of how the ride could possibly go.

Then it was our turn. My husband gently grabbed my hand and led me onto the ride—or to my death, as I saw it. I climbed on, shaking as I took breaths more rapidly. I started to cry as they told us to pull the safety harness over our shoulders. The people next to us saw how upset I was. They tried to encourage me; it wasn't all that bad. There was also a lady who was standing in line waiting her turn and she could see how upset I was. I knew she was shouting within, "Someone please get this poor girl off of this roller coaster." But they didn't.

"Alright, everyone, are you ready for this ride? If you are ready, scream woohoo!" the conductor shouted.

I was freaking out. My hands were tingling; I could barely feel them. My legs were trembling.

The ride cranked towards the peak faster and faster, matching my heartbeat. Eventually, the cranking stopped, and I am pretty sure my heart did as well. Just my luck, rain started to fall (awesome, more obstacles).

After a long pause, we started our descent.

A huge rush came over my body, but it wasn't what I expected. I couldn't believe what I was experiencing. The rush I was feeling wasn't terror or panic. My body was full of adrenaline, joy, and excitement! We whipped around, went upside down, and I screamed with considerable release and freedom!

When the ride came to a screeching halt, I looked over at my husband with a surprised look on my face and admitted, "That really wasn't that bad. I think I actually liked it!"

The people next to us reminded me, "See, we told you it wasn't horrible and that you would like it!"

I rode six roller coasters that day. Six! I was proud of myself, and I had a blast. I wanted to ride them over and over again.

Although I admit, there was this one roller coaster I will *never* ride again called the Cobra Strike; it didn't have shoulder harnesses and it went upside down. I felt like I was going to fall out of my seat. Never again!

There was also a roller coaster there I was absolutely not going to ride, and to be honest I may never ride it.

The ride was called Fury 325. The Fury 325 is the world's tallest and fastest roller coaster. The highest point is 325 feet in the air with a maximum speed of 95 miles per hour. The track is over a mile long.

My husband jokingly pointed to it, "You want to ride that one?" (You mean the one that has a flashing light on the top of it so that airplanes won't hit it?)

I quickly divulged, "I am not there yet! And I do not know if I will ever be."

"And it is okay, babe! Look around at all you overcame today!"

Homeschool is a *crazy* ride; a ride I never thought I would be on. When I was faced with the idea of it, I did not want to get on it. I was reluctant, terrified, and I cried for weeks after saying yes to it. But it has turned out that the ride I did not want to be on, has over time become my absolute favorite of all time.

My final confession: I love homeschool!

MY FINAL CONFESSION: I LOVE HOMESCHOOL!

Yes, our homeschool journey has been an emotional roller-coaster! On our homeschool journey, there have been many ups and downs, twists, and turns. There have been moments of panic and peace. There have been moments of laughter and praise, fears, and tears. There have been moments of pushing through and countless moments of "I quit!"

But you want to know a secret? I wouldn't change it for the world. I know now homeschool is a gift; a gift I often take for granted.

Every day is a new journey, a new ride, which we get the opportunity to be a part of together as a family. Every day I get a front-row seat to the lives of our boys. Not only that, but when discouragement or fear does try to trip up our boys, when they realize they haven't quite arrived, my husband and I get to hold their hands and say, "It is okay you aren't there yet; neither are we. But let's look around at all we overcame *today*."

○ ○ ○

Tips For Success #11:
Enjoy the Ride

I have no idea the circumstances which brought you and your family to this place of homeschooling your children.

I do not know if you are doing it on your own or with a spouse. I don't know if you are a working mother, a stay-at-home mom, or both. I do not know if you are terrified or if you are excited about the journey you are on. I don't know if you are just starting out or if you have been at the homeschool game for a long time. I don't know if you are homeschooling for a season or if you are in it for the long haul.

Whatever the circumstances surrounding your homeschool life, I want to encourage you to enjoy the ride. In each moment of faith or fear, of peace or panic, confidence, or lack thereof; I want to encourage you to take a deep breath, throw your hands up in the air, let joy in, and shout with release and freedom.

Enjoy it momma; homeschooling is a gift!

So keep on going. Don't quit! You can absolutely do this. God brought you and your family to this place for a reason, for a purpose. Don't rush it, don't become frantic in it, just take the days and the moments as they come and do all you can to learn from every single one of them; the good, the bad, and the ugly.

I believe in you, momma. Now, throw your shoulders back, lift up your head, breathe in confidence, breathe out skepticism, and believe in yourself!

You've got this!

Prayer:
Lord, I know you have brought my family to this place of homeschooling for a purpose. I pray in my moments of doubt, fear, and panic you remind me of the gift I have in homeschooling our children, and fill my heart and mind with confidence, faith, and peace. I pray when I don't believe I can do it anymore, you would remind me I can—by leaning on your strength and not my own. I pray when I do not feel like I am enough as a mom and a homeschool mom that you remind me, I am enough. Lord, help me to trust you in this process no matter what may come our way. Help me to enjoy the journey.

In Jesus' Name,
Amen

> Psalm 3:3, "But You, Lord, are a shield around me, my glory, and the One who lifts up my head."

> Psalm 16:11, "You reveal the path of life to me; in Your presence is abundant joy; in Your right hand are eternal pleasures.

> Psalm 119:105, "Your word is a lamp for my feet and a light on my path."

Psalm 118:24, "This is the day the LORD has made; let us rejoice and be glad in it."

2 Timothy 1:7, "For God has not given us a spirit of fearfulness, but one of power, love, and sound judgment."

Don't Give Up

I want to challenge you to write an encouraging letter to yourself so when all the doubts and insecurities come, and they will, you can come back to this place. Stay encouraged momma, and don't lose heart!

_____

_____

_____

_____

_____

_____

_____

_____

_____

_____

_____

_____

_____

Fill Up Your Bookshelf

Things to do to make sure homeschool stays your favorite:

1. Spend time with the Lord daily (get into the Word, worship, pray).
2. Create a homeschool mission statement with your family and post it where you can all see it every single day.
3. Reach out to a handful of people who will pray for you and your family as you homeschool.
4. Reach out to a handful of people and ask them to randomly reach out to you and encourage you on your journey. These people can be the same people who you have asked to pray for you or a totally different set of people.
5. Encourage others on their homeschool journey. When we encourage other people, it is amazing how we ourselves will be encouraged to keep going.
6. Pray for other homeschool families.
7. Find an outlet. Everyone needs a break from the pressures of life and that includes you. Find something that brings you a reprieve and schedule it into your routine.
8. Laugh at your mistakes because you will make them, and it is better to brush them off than to dwell on them.
9. No matter what—and I cannot stress this enough—maintain a *teachable spirit* and encourage your children to as well. We can always learn from others around us. On the same token other people can learn from us, but if we walk around like know-it-alls no one will ever care to listen. We need to remind and encourage ourselves and our kids that there is always space to learn. And we as parents have to remember that we can always learn something new—even if it is from our kids.
10. Don't make your entire life *all* about homeschool; there is more to life.

DON'T QUIT!
Homeschool Your Children with Confidence
YOU'VE GOT THIS!

Author's Note

Momma,

If I were sitting with you chatting over a hot cup of coffee, I would put my coffee down and give you the biggest hug ever! I want you to know that you are a fantastic mom! You are beautiful, capable, strong—and I want you to know that you can absolutely do this homeschool thing.

I do not want you to view homeschool as a massive, frightening monster that cannot be tamed. Yes, homeschool can be stressful sometimes but there is so much beauty and freedom in it. Take the moments–the good, the bad, and the ugly–as they come and use them as opportunities for growth instead of seeing them as burdensome.

These moments with your children are fleeting. So, allow yourself to slow down and enjoy every single breath with them. Laugh with them, play with them, do things with them that they enjoy, and as my oldest brother has always encouraged me, "Hug em' while you can." Your kids need you and your love more than you will ever know!

Take each day, each moment at a time—and continue to breathe in confidence and breathe out skepticism.

You've got this, momma!

You are not alone!

Find me on social media—or visit my website—and hang out with me there for additional information and encouragement.

@TiffanyWassonAuthor
@TiffanyWassonAuthor
Website: TiffanyWasson.com

Your Cheerleader,
Tiffany

A List of Homeschool Must-Haves

Here are some favorites, must-haves, and survival tips from other homeschool moms and me. These are things that you don't necessarily have to have or do but they have all made homeschooling so much easier and more enjoyable for every single mom who contributed to this list.

1. Dance Breaks: They breathe life into our days.
2. Laughter: We don't always have to be so serious.
3. Coffee: Lots and lots of coffee/tea.
4. Laminator: I found a cheap one on amazon and it has revolutionized our organization.
5. Calendar.
6. Lesson Plans: Create one that what works best for your family.
7. Quiet Time Out: When everyone goes to their own rooms.
8. Exercise: It is easy to sit too much in homeschool so get those bodies moving.
9. Time to sit together without a pen or pencil... read together.
10. Grace: If it gets done it gets done...even if they are doing it upside down.
11. Everyone has their own set of things (paper, dry erase markers, crayons, pencils, color pencils...anything to keep the peace).

12. Field Trips.
13. Family Vacations.
14. Sabbath: Every week, at least one day, and then every seven weeks for a week. It is so easy to feel guilty in homeschool when breaks are taken but they are so necessary. Breathe in rest, breathe out the guilt.
15. Time together each day that doesn't involve school. Just be their mom and listen.
16. Mentors, other than you, whom you can trust to pour into your kids.
17. Educational films: On the hard days, it is nice to have these on hand. Not only does it provide a break but learning still happens.
18. Their favorite book: They need a break from pure educational reading. Give them a book they enjoy, and they will devour it and learn by accident.
19. Learning Board Games: There are so many games out there you can use to take a break with your kids, have fun, and still be learning.
20. Creative time: Draw, paint, come up with a short story together.

Encouraging Words From Other Moms

"The best advice I ever received about homeschooling came from a dear friend who mentored me in my homeschool journey. She told me, 'Remember, you bought the curriculum; it didn't buy you.' This gave me the freedom to know that my daughters didn't have to do every problem on every page of every chapter. If a particular curriculum wasn't working for someone, we could change in midstream and find one that worked. I'd also like to add that community is vital, even if it has to be virtual. Lone Ranger homeschooling is tough. Make the effort to find community."

Susan, Homeschool Mom of Twenty-Five Years

"When we decided to homeschool our three boys, we considered the benefits and all the beautiful things about homeschooling, but without personal experience, we didn't anticipate the days that were not so beautiful. To the momma who is facing those harder days: Stay the course! When feelings of doubt are creeping in, and you've entered a season of struggle, just know you have not failed! In those difficult times, you experience the most growth. God called you to teach and train your children in the instruction of the Lord, and He will sustain you through *all* the hard seasons! I can tell you from experience, with multiple children there can be many! But seasons change and there are good fruits, which are yielded at harvest! Don't compare where you are right now, to anyone else! The Lord has planned your journey, and the Holy Spirit is your guide!"

Haley, Homeschool Mom of Ten Years

"We started homeschooling to fill a need my children's public school was not able to fill. As time went by, I slowly realized I might just be in over my head. Did I make a mistake? Was public school really that bad for my kids? How was I ever going to do this? Then came that still, soft voice. God reassured me and continues to reassure me that, time and time again He is the center of it all. He was the one who would get me through those rough mornings that I wish I could just send them back to school. He was the one who lifted my heart up when I felt down, defeated, or deflated. He was the one who was ultimately responsible for each of these beautiful children I was working so hard to care for. He is the center of it all and should absolutely be the center of this homeschooling journey for you, too. Momma, you can do this."

Victoria, Homeschool Mom of Four Years

"This week my husband thanked me for homeschooling our children. He said that after ten years he can truly see what it has done for them. I can't say that either of my children loves school, but they love learning and they've learned how to learn. More than anything, they've been filled with biblical knowledge and have had many deep philosophical conversations with us over the years because we're simply together all the time. Homeschooling has changed our whole family for the better!"

Ginger, Homeschool Mom of Ten Years

"Pray, then trust Him with your kids. Trust Him to lead you. Trust Him to provide the right friends and experiences for your kids. Remember that He loves your children more than you do and He knows what He is doing by calling you to homeschool. Be faithful and work hard, even when you can't see the fruit of your labor yet. You will in time. He is a faithful, faithful God! 1 Chronicles 28:20 says, 'Be strong and courageous, and do the work. Don't be afraid or discouraged, for the LORD God, my God, is with you' (NIV)."

Charity, Homeschool Mom of Fourteen Years

"I believe the hardest but best lesson I've learned is simply to trust God's plan. When I first began our homeschool journey, I compared my children's progress and daily routines (usually the negative parts only!) to other families. I worried so much I wasn't doing enough or failing my kids somehow. It wasn't until I went to a homeschool convention, and heard a seasoned mom confess the same fears, that I knew God saw differently. She shared God spoke to her and asked her, 'Who called you to homeschool?' 'You did, God!' Then she said He gently and lovingly told her, 'Then trust me to carry My plan out.' Hearing those words confirmed in me that God was doing the same for my family. He called us to homeschool. He was in control. I just continue to trust in Him every day, and I encourage you to do the same."

Kim, Homeschool Mom of Eight Years

"Homeschooling was never a part of my plan. We are a military family and move frequently. My oldest was in first grade and within a month I found out I was pregnant with our fourth baby and that we were moving after only one year. I felt like I was drowning and in the middle of the chaos, we felt God calling us to homeschool. I didn't think it was possible, but

God! Homeschooling is hard but so worth it. Now, many years later, I am seeing my oldest children thrive because of all the years of learning how to learn! When things feel hard and overwhelming, pray and remember *who* called you to do this and *what* is important. And don't forget to make time for yourself, so you can better serve your family. This will encourage your precious children to remember what matters most."

Jessica, Homeschool Mom of Nine Years

"As moms, we go-go-go and think we have to have everything done and done to perfection and when we fail at perfection, we blame ourselves. I have been homeschooling for eight years now and here are a few things I've learned along the way:

1. If it's not working, try something new.
There are so many options for curriculum out there and this can be both intimidating and exciting. Maybe you are looking at homeschooling, just starting out, or a veteran homeschooler looking for new ways of doing things, I would encourage you to read *The Everything Guide to Homeschooling*. This book has helped me over the years in so many ways.

2. Go with the flow!
I am a very organized person and have my year planned out almost nine months in advance, but it *never* goes as planned. Life happens and you have to roll with it. Even if your kids are in public or private school, they won't complete every task planned. In fact, most kids in school only complete about half to three-fourths of the course before the end of the year. That is one of the reasons why the first two-to-three months of school are a review of the previous year. It is great

to have a plan to keep things on track, and if you live in a more restricted state this is a huge help, but remember everyone has sick days. Maybe the plan changes and instead of the worksheet of math you choose to bake or build something to apply those math skills to real life. Remember education isn't just knowing facts, it's knowing how to use those facts in the real world.

3. We can't do it all!
It is okay to ask for help from family, friends, homeschool community, and more. I am not a teacher and I stink at history and language arts, but God blessed me with a husband who is awesome at both, and I take full advantage of that. Maybe you just feel overwhelmed and need some help yourself. Again, seek advice from people you trust and be okay with asking for help in whatever area you feel you could use it.

4. Find your outlet!
When we add 'teacher' to our mom resume it can be overwhelming at times no matter who you are. It is so important for us to find our space to recharge. It can be gardening, photography, taking a walk, shopping with a friend, whatever you find that gives you kid-free time. Don't feel bad about yourself when you need the time. I can't tell you how many moms I have heard losing their minds because their kids are off for a week for Spring break....I always want to say, 'try it full-time, 365 days a year' but I don't.

5. Remember why you chose this lifestyle!
In the craziness of life, when we feel overwhelmed and want to throw in the towel and say, 'I'm done,' stop, take a deep breath, and remember why you felt it was best to teach your children at home. Maybe it was religious, maybe it was

to help a child with special needs get the education they deserve, maybe it was because of safety concerns, whatever the reason, remember it and focus on that. Take the rest of that day off, do something with your kids that will build your relationship, and fight the handwriting battle tomorrow. You can do this!"

Crystal, Homeschool Mom of Eight Years

"In our early years of homeschooling, I found myself getting so caught up with the standards of those around me that I was stretching myself and my kids to a thin line. Not only was it causing stress in our school time, but in our family time as well. I put myself in this 'perfectly' squared box. Why was I so focused on all the structure and standards set by others and public school!? I chose to homeschool because of the freedom! When I stopped comparing, that's when my true self was able to shine through. It's one of the most self-rewarding aspects of homeschooling! Allowing ourselves to be given grace just as we give grace to our children. We have been blessed with the ability to be at home with our children as well as be their full-time educators. We are setting their morals and values with an excellent foundation! On those hard days don't give up, instead shift your focus, and get outside of your comfort zone to shake things up. Homeschooling isn't just pen and paper. Get out there and experience what the world has to offer, *together*. You'll be so glad you did!"

Lesley, Homeschool Mom of Six Years

"Whenever we have a hard day, I step back and look at all we have been able to do and accomplish. Our children have all created such sweet relationships with each other as well as the Lord. I love that God has called us into this life I never planned for; we have been blessed with family time, growth, and flexibility whenever we most needed it. Being able to homeschool is often challenging but we know we are better at equipping our children for life and the world that awaits them. I thank God every day for giving me strength, grace, patience, and love to carry out His plan."

Sierra, Homeschool Mom of Six Years

"Homeschooling is hard...but then again parenting is hard. I have found that if I can get back in touch with what I really want for my children...to have curious children who love to learn...then I am freer to help them develop their God-given gifts, talents, and passions. It's a constant struggle to choose out of the trap of comparing my kids to other people's kids and to turn away from what our world defines as success. At times I have screamed, cried, and threatened to send them to school, but I wouldn't trade these years for anything, because God has grown me in ways, I never imagined...closer to my children and closer to the heart of God."

Mary, Homeschool Mom of Nine Years

"Before you start your school day, pray. Pray over the state of your heart and the hearts of your children. For grace, peace, and mercy and the daily bread sufficient for the day."

Cassidy, Homeschool Mom of Three Years

Encouraging Words From Kids

"Homeschool is super fun once you get used to it and get into your personal groove. All you have to do is try to find ways to make the hard things more fun. Homeschool is comfortable because you get to stay wrapped up in blankets with hot cocoa on cold days."

Aaron, Age Twelve

"The good part of homeschool is that I get to spend every day with my family. My favorite part about homeschool is that I get to cuddle with my mom while reading a book. Homeschool is really fun so do not give up! If you want to quit, don't do that! Keep on trying."

Austin, Age Ten

"Homeschool allows you a flexible schedule and the ability to learn from a Christian worldview."

Denton, Age Sixteen

"Push through! It will be better for them in the long run."

Braydon, Age Ten

"Your kids will get a better education with real-life skills included."

Eliana, Age Thirteen

"Don't quit when it gets hard. We like homeschooling more than we say."

Bella, Age Eleven

"I love homeschooling instead of going to public school a lot. I have the ability to work at my own pace and focus on the subjects that interest me more like science and Latin. Homeschooling also allows me to have more time to read, get outside, and hang out with my family. I enjoy homeschooling very much."

Scarlett, Age Twelve

"I like homeschooling because I can go at my own pace so there is more time to read and play. Homeschool also helps work on your child's weak points because you can focus on spending more time (or less time) on different subjects. If you want to quit homeschool don't give up! But in the end, it is your decision."

Zachary, Age 10

"I love getting to learn with my brothers and sister, we get more time to play and explore together. If you ever want to quit just keep going and doing homeschool, it's good for your kids."

Maxwell, Age Seven

"I love learning with my mama and being home with her and my brothers and sister."

Alexander, Age Four

"Even though I've never been to public school, I think it's a lot more fun to be homeschooled because I like being home to see my parents and my siblings. I think it will be more fun for you too."

Everett, Age Ten

"It's really fun being homeschooled. I like to study the work I am given, and I think this is because I am homeschooled. I think your kids might like it too."

Bentley, Age Fourteen

"It will make a difference in you and your kids' lives."

Aspen, Age Seventeen

"Homeschooling is the perfect way to teach your kids the way you believe they deserve to be taught and push them the way you think they should be pushed. You get to show them God's love throughout their journey and help them to learn real-life skills and better prepare them for adulthood."

Cami, Age Sixteen

Acknowledgments

F riends, I honestly cannot believe this is my second book. I am shocked! I never saw myself as a writer and now to be an author of two books seems like a dream (someone pinch me)! There is absolutely no way this book would exist today if it wasn't for the faithfulness of God and so many others who helped me see this project through to the very end.

To Donald Newman at Xulon Press, your continual support and encouragement is like no other and I would not be where I am today without you! Not only do you make me better by simply being who you are, but you have also helped me to dream impossible dreams again and see them through until they are a reality. Thank you!

To the rest of the Xulon Press team, every single one of you are fantastic people! You go above and beyond the call of duty to make sure stories of people like me are put out there to help change the world. All your work does not go unnoticed! Thank you!

To my editor Brittnee Taylor, thank you for saying yes to being my editor! My book is on a whole other level because of your drive, care, and attentiveness. Seriously, thank you!

To my dear friends Anthony and Brittany Rodd, thank you for your time, patience, and willingness to take *as many pictures* as needed to make the cover of this book as perfect as possible. Also, thank you for helping me with my launch video! I had a blast working with you both and I am so thankful for the two of you! Also, you guys make me better!

To sweet hospitable Kristina Teal, thank you for welcoming Anthony, Brittany, and me into your home to take pictures for the front cover. Your home is gorgeous, and the front cover is all that it is today because of you. Thank you!

To The Beautiful Mess Photography, thank you for capturing the most perfect picture for my author photo. I am so thankful that time and time again, you have been able to capture the most precious moments of my kids and I that I will cherish forever.

To my Input Family, Launch Team, and Read Team, thank you for all your advice, your time, and willingness to help make this book all it is today. You all made me think of things and see things I would have never noticed. You were also one of the main reasons I kept on going! There were so many times I wanted to quit writing this book.

To all the mommas who helped me during this process, thank you! I know by asking you to write encouraging notes and have your children write encouraging notes was a lot to ask with all your hectic schedules. All of you are my superheroes! Thank you for your time and willingness to help! And thank you for always keeping me on my toes by asking me, "Is your book done yet?"

To my fellow "dream chaser" Victoria Wilson, thank you for being my compass. You have kept me so focused on my dreams through your prayers, conversations, and encouragement. You are the truly the most amazing friend a girl could ever have! Not only do I love our friendship, but I know that this book would have never been finished if it wasn't for you. I am so thankful for you! Oh, and Victoria, "You chase that dream!"

To my husband Jeremy Wasson, thank you for always being my biggest fan and for always encouraging me to chase after my crazy dreams. Your belief in me and your love for me puts wind in my sails. You help me more than you will ever know! You are my calm, my comic relief, my encouragement when I want to give up, and my best friend. You are my forever date, my kitchen dance partner, and my "bust out in old people music person" to annoy our kid's. You are the one who still makes my heart skip a beat after all these years. You are the love of my life. I am so glad God had our paths cross! I love you so much and I am so thankful that we are in this life together.

To our boys Aaron and Austin, thank you for also being big fans of mommy. You hilariously tell people to buy my books wherever we go. Your support is the greatest. Also, not only are you the main reason for me writing this book but you are the main reasons I never want to give up on my dreams. I want you to know that no matter what your dreams are in life, to run after them until you see them come to fulfillment. I believe in you both and I love you both!

To my parents Larry and Kristin Williams, thank you for all the talks, all your encouragement, and back and forth about this book. I have no idea what I would do without the two of you! Not only did you help me so much during this process, but you help me so much in my life! You are both treasures to me and I hope you never forget that fact! There are not enough words to say how much I appreciate you. I love you both so much!

To my brothers and sisters, Todd, Travis, Trent, Kristen, Inga, Paige, and Brooke, thank you for being my rocks during the crazy year we have had. We have all been through so much, but I am so thankful that I have all of you to lean on. I am thankful that I am not alone in this crazy life. I love you all!

To my mom Judy Mason, I miss you more than words can say. I hate you are no longer with us, but I know you are in a much better place. Every single time I wanted to give up on this project, all the encouraging words which you have spoken to me over the years would come to my mind. I know where I am today is a product of all your encouragement and prayers. I am so grateful for you mom, and I love you!

To Jesus, you are my center. I cannot live, move, or breathe without you. You are my everything, and I am nothing without you!